Praise for *Don't Let School Get in the Way of Education*

"As a personal success coach who once served as a teacher in the Chicago Public Schools, I can attest with conviction that this book belongs in the professional development toolkit of every educator. It not only explains the underachievement of America's youth but also offers specific solutions to promote their success in school and in life. Through his insight and creativity, Olatunji provides a much-needed paradigm shift for improving the way we teach and learn."

—**Jack Canfield,** coauthor, Chicken Soup for the Soul® series and *The Success Principles*™; author, *Self-Esteem in the Classroom*

"Olatunji not only captures the sources of student disengagement in schools but also provides specific, evidence-supported strategies to engage and motivate young learners. This inspirational, practical, and well-informed work is clearly a valuable resource for classroom teachers at every level and for educational administrators and policy makers. The book is also enjoyable to read and accessible, and I recommend it to educators everywhere."

—**Richard M. Ryan,** professor, Institute for Positive Psychology and Education, Australian Catholic University

"Beginning with the premise that ALL students have the talent and potential to succeed, Dr. Olatunji inspires instructors to become culturally validating educators and to address not only academic competencies but also inner life skills such as self-awareness and sense of purpose. This is an inspiring, innovative book for all educators who are looking for a new way to improve academic success and the overall wellness of our nation's youth."

—**Laura I. Rendón;** professor emerita, University of Texas at San Antonio; author, *Sentipensante (Sensing/Thinking) Pedagogy: Educating for Wholeness, Social Justice, and Liberation*

"In this engaging read, Dr. Olatunji weaves together evidence and stories for an education approach he calls FACES: Fun, Affirmation, Challenge, Expression, and Success. I particularly appreciate his use of easy-to-grasp metaphors and numerous examples that make key education theories such as self-determination, intrinsic and extrinsic motivation, and the learning sciences accessible to readers, especially parents. Part memoir, part education theory for a general audience, and part call to action, this book is all heart."

—**Rebecca E. Wolfe,** vice president of impact and improvement and senior advisor of network and engagement, KnowledgeWorks, Inc.

"This book wonderfully explains why a better way of education is needed. It is beautifully written in language that is understandable for parents, teachers, and broad audiences. A work well done and necessary!!"

—**Kassie Freeman,** senior faculty research fellow, Edmund W. Gordon Institute for Advanced Study, Teachers College, Columbia University

"This is a must-read from a passionate scholar and educator."

—**Tony Nicholas Brown,** distinguished professor of sociology, Rice University

"Through his own work and experience, lessons shared by others, and research, Dr. Olatunji articulates the difference between schooling and education. He maps a path to success for teachers and learners through knowledge and understanding (not just testing), curiosity and questioning (not just following instructions), and engagement and relationships (not just passing through). More than ever, we as educators need to find multiple ways and multiple spheres in which to engage and empower students to achieve the dream of a knowledgeable, well-educated, and equitable society—making this book essential reading for our time."

—**Ethan Yazzie-Mintz;** cofounder and executive director, First Light Education Project; former director, High School Survey of Student Engagement, Indiana University

DON'T LET SCHOOL GET IN THE WAY OF EDUCATION

HOW TO IMPROVE *the* PERFORMANCE *and* WELL-BEING *of* OUR NATION'S YOUTH

ANANE N. OLATUNJI, PhD

RIVER GROVE
BOOKS

The author of this book comments on, compares, and criticizes models and theories generally pertaining to K-12 and college-level models of educational instruction. The author's opinions expressed herein are based on his personal experiences, observations, and research on the subject matter. The author's opinions may not be universally applicable to all people in all circumstances. Some names have been changed to protect privacy. The information provided within this book is for general informational and educational purposes only. The author of this book disclaims liability for any loss or damage suffered by any person as a result of the information or content in this book. **The author expressly prohibits any entity from using this publication to train AI technologies to generate text or photos or for ML purposes**, including, without limitation, technologies capable of generating textual, photographic, or other works in the same style or genre as this publication.

Published by River Grove Books
Austin, TX
www.rivergrovebooks.com

Copyright © 2025 Anane N. Olatunji

All rights reserved.

For more information, go to the author's website at DrOinspires.com.

Thank you for purchasing an authorized edition of this book and for complying with copyright law. No part of this book may be reproduced, stored in a retrieval system, or transmitted by any means, electronic, mechanical, photocopying, recording, or otherwise, without written permission from the copyright holder.

Distributed by River Grove Books

Design and composition by Greenleaf Book Group
Cover design by Greenleaf Book Group

Publisher's Cataloging-in-Publication data is available.

Print ISBN: 978-1-63299-961-0

eBook ISBN: 978-1-63299-962-7

First Edition

This book is dedicated to the memory of Edmund Evans Perry (1967–1985) and to all youth so that they might thrive.

Contents

Preface xi

Introduction 1

PART I

Chapter 1. The Broccoli Model of Education 17

Chapter 2. Education Dilemma: Academic Rigor versus Emotional Well-Being 35

Chapter 3. Common Core Consequences of Conventional Education 57

Chapter 4. Reality Check: Insights from School Leaders . . . 75

Chapter 5. A New Paradigm for Education 87

PART II

Chapter 6. Fun: Enjoyment of Learning 109

Chapter 7. Affirmation: "I Like It When You Call Me Teresita!" 125

Chapter 8. Challenge: Using Connection and Direction . . 149

Chapter 9. Expression: Cultivating Autonomy and Agency. . 167

Chapter 10. Success: Principles for Prosperity 181

Conclusion 197

Support the Mission 207

Acknowledgments 209

Notes 211

Index 231

About the Author 239

Preface

And God said, Let there be light: and there was light. And God saw the light, that it was good: and God divided the light from the darkness.

—Genesis 1:3–4 (KJV)

As far back as I can remember, all the adults in my life extolled the virtues of education. My parents, relatives, teachers, and mentors all inculcated in me, from the earliest days of my childhood to young adulthood, the idea that education was the gateway to success. Now, reflecting on six decades of life experience, it may seem ironic coming from a successful Ivy Leaguer, but I must respectfully yet unapologetically disagree.

Not until the second half of my life did I discover that there was something much more important to achieving success than the knowledge, skills, and credentials conferred by formal education. The great quest for fulfillment in life comes to us not by the accumulation of things from without but within. Thus, I believe that one cannot achieve success without a sense of spiritual wholeness. And that state can only be attained through congruence between how we see ourselves, how we see the world, and what we do in it. Otherwise, life becomes fragmented and painful.

Therein lies the disconnect between the process of education (schooling) and the goal of life: self-actualization. Contrary to all that I learned as a child, life has taught me that conventional education is not the key. Moreover, at times, such education even obscures the key. By conventional education, I mean schooling and academic credentialing as commonly practiced in the United States and in much of the world.

That being said, allow me to clarify this point so as not to leave you with the erroneous impression that I am anything other than a staunch education advocate. Having reaped tremendous benefits from education in my own career, I strongly believe it is one of the best investments anyone can make for future prosperity. So, I encourage all students to increase their knowledge, acquire new skills, and earn whatever credentials they may need.

On the other hand, along my journey, I have observed and experienced how schooling can sometimes obstruct the path to success. When this occurs, then education actually impedes the very outcome it was designed to promote. To that extent, education has a lot in common with money; both are good as long as having or pursuing them doesn't jeopardize one's well-being overall. So, while I strongly encourage youth to get an education, understand this: For achieving success, self-knowledge is indispensable because it determines how well one uses their education. To put it another way, the core subjects of reading and math are important, but never lose sight of the ultimate subject—the student.

Unfortunately, self-knowledge is like a seed that often fails to take root, either because it remains hidden or lost along life's journey. For most children, school is a major part of that journey. Thus, I have written this book first to enlighten the path so that more youth might succeed—in school and beyond. To that end, this book explains why a better way of education is needed and how to make that vision a reality.

Introduction

"Hey! Wassup, Teach?" "Hola! Cómo estás?" "Are you our new teacher today? I can help you!"

Those were among the greetings I heard on my first day as a substitute teacher waiting in the hallway for class to begin at a public junior high school in New York City. "SEEN-suh-mi-lee-uh! SEEN-suh-mi-lee-uh!" blurted a young male student as he sashayed briskly down the aisle with one hand tucked in his pocket.

Understanding him to mean *sinsemilla* marijuana, I thought, *Okay . . . this is going to be interesting.* The bell rang and class commenced with an ethnic medley of about twenty-eight seventh graders seated in front of me. They were abuzz with excitement like paparazzi at a red-carpet event. As for me, at age twenty-six, I felt energetic yet overwhelmed.

The tone of my ninth-grade classroom that afternoon, however, was precisely the opposite. For starters, this class had far fewer students, only about fifteen. They were lethargic rather than excited, sagging into their seats as though ill. Instead of curiosity and enthusiasm, apathy and anxiety tainted their faces. They seemed interested only in how soon the bell would ring to liberate them from my oversight. *Is this,* I thought, *what happens to kids at this school between seventh and ninth grades?*

Later that same week, during lunch in the faculty lounge, I listened in on a heated conversation among teachers about the challenges of their profession. The words exclaimed by one male teacher remain imprinted on my mind to this day: "Next to parenting, this is the most important job in the world!" Those words made me want to know more. Why were the attitudes between my seventh- and ninth-grade students so drastically different? Why were the older kids so apathetic, so lifeless?

This book addresses that perplexing and persistent problem in education. Although its effects are often more obvious among older youth, ethnic minorities, and the economically disadvantaged, the problem impacts young people from all social backgrounds. Due to its subtle nature, however, many people are not even aware of its existence. Yet, some who are aware don't consider it a problem at all. Just like with the COVID-19 virus, many seem to think that so long as most kids appear to be all right, there's nothing to worry about. That pandemic-like problem is—alienation from school.

By alienation from school, I mean that young people are disconnected emotionally from school. Therefore, they don't invest enough of themselves into it, and consequently, they get far too little from it in return. Thus, education, which should be an amazingly engaging and fulfilling experience of personal growth and self-development, ends up merely as preparation for a life of mediocrity. What a waste of human potential!

As subtle a problem as it may be, considerable research substantiates the extensiveness as well as the severity of alienation from school among adolescents. In a five-year series of national surveys, two out of every three high school students said they are bored in class every . . . single . . . day. When asked, "Why?" most responded that the "material wasn't interesting [or] relevant to me."[1] But if that alone doesn't make the case, consider the following:

- The longer kids stay in school, the less engaged they become.[2]
- Even in private schools renowned for academic excellence, 83 percent of students say they are bored.[3]
- One of the main reasons students give for dropping out of school is that they don't like it.[4]

And, as you might imagine, what happens in high school naturally impacts education at the next level. Among college students, for example, the overall dropout rate of 39 percent is much higher than in high school.[5] And although students most often say that they leave for financial reasons, a combination of academic and social challenges accounts for an even larger share of those who drop out.[6]

Just like compounded interest that grows over time, the consequences of alienation from school eventually accrue right into the workforce. First, because they spent so much time focusing on academic subjects, many young people graduate without a clue as to what they'd actually like to do with their lives. Consequently, they become even more lost by looking for a "good job" instead of the "right job." Second, school's focus on academic knowledge neglects attention to real-world experiences that would equip youth with a sense of direction prior to entering the workforce. Third, and perhaps worst of all, those who do get employment join a workforce where most find their jobs unfulfilling.[7] Welcome, boys and girls, to the rat race!

Alienation thus breeds underperformance—in high school, college, and in the workforce. And this underperformance, in turn, no longer undermines prosperity just for the individual, but also for the society awaiting their contribution. Does that sound even close to an equation for personal success and prosperity? Unfortunately, we have grown accustomed to this mediocrity to the point where we don't even recognize it. That might be the way it is, but can we do better? Of course! We can, we should, we must.

I believe that two fundamental flaws in the conventional education system are to blame for this far-reaching problem. First, school tends to be too academic or abstract. In general, it teaches in ways that seem to have little or nothing to do with reality. By separating education from real life, school becomes irrelevant and thus alienating to students. Second, school's emphasis on academic skills minimizes the undeniably important role that emotion plays in performance. Underlying school's neglect of feelings is the unspoken yet powerful idea that intelligence is the key to success. Or, to put it in "educationese," *Cognition is king!*

Look, however, at the highest achievers in any field and you'll see that passion is essential to their performance. Regarded by many as the greatest boxer of all time, Muhammad Ali once said:

> Champions are made from something they
> have deep inside them—a desire, a dream, a
> vision. . . . They have to have the skill, and the will.
> But the will must be stronger than the skill.[8]

We must close the gap between school and the real world. I believe schools can teach knowledge and skills without compromising zeal and zest. They can promote high levels of academic achievement and, at the same time, inspire emotional fulfillment. Those ends are not mutually exclusive. To close that gap, however, we need to see education through the eyes of young people and with open minds and hearts.

A New Paradigm

With the success and prosperity of our young people in mind, this book offers advocates a solution to the problem of alienation from school. I've developed this solution over the course of my career, especially the eight years I spent as a teacher. I call the model or framework FACES, which stands for: Fun, Affirmation, Challenge, Expression, and Success. The framework is as practical as it is symbolic. School should be a place where students get to see and feel themselves at the center of the educational process, as subjects rather than objects of instruction. In this book, I'll show you how to implement each of these five features. And you will see that FACES provides the field of education with what it unknowingly needs most: a facelift, a paradigm shift.

This book is about the *faces behind the numbers* (GPA, SAT, and whatever tests your state uses). I contend that schools should move *away* from education driven by test scores and *toward* emotional fulfillment. That's right, emotional fulfillment. That goes beyond the concept of emotional wellness. What I'm advocating here is that we take it up a notch or two. Let's transform education by making school a place that not only recognizes the individual talents and interests of students, but also fosters their development. In short, the FACES framework advocates that we switch the predominant educational paradigm from "Cognition is king!" to "Passion propels performance!" Why? Because passion—not intellect—is the fuel of human achievement.

Ever noticed how Mother Nature herself abides by this same principle? To ensure our survival as a species, she made the process of procreation not a mind-numbing obligation but an enjoyable experience emotionally. Why not follow her wisdom when it comes to reforming education?

The Promise

Now pause for a moment and think about the implications of what I've just described. If schools operated from a paradigm based on emotional fulfillment rather than cognitive development, then we would see student engagement *increase* over the course of schooling rather than decline. Imagine! Indeed, that would truly be a game changer. Why? Because such a paradigm shift would align the educational process with human nature. The need for meaningful activity is fundamental to us as human beings, isn't it? Unfortunately, students have made clear that this need is all too often frustrated in school.

By channeling the energy of emotion into their work, students will not only get higher grades and test scores but also a more fulfilling education in general. If in college, they will not only get more out of the experience but also a satisfying job after graduating. High school administrators who use the principles herein will see not only increases in their graduation and college admissions rates, but their students will also finish high school with a greater sense of purpose and direction. For the same reasons, college and university educators can expect higher retention and graduation rates. Regardless of the educational level, this book will help young people to become more successful—in school and in life. And while I certainly don't mean to suggest that it contains the solution to every problem in education, I can promise you that by applying the book's principles, your children, or the youth you serve, will be much more likely to become happy, healthy high achievers.

I invite you then to join me on this journey. We'll start out in chapter 1, The Broccoli Model of Education, by surveying where we are in education today, two decades and counting into the twenty-first century. We'll listen to what students themselves have to say about this topic, as well as to the experts. In chapter 2, Education Dilemma: Academic Rigor versus Emotional Well-Being, we'll take a nosedive and learn from the actual experience of one adolescent's tragic story to see how deep the potential perils of conventional education can go. In chapter 3, Common Core Consequences of Conventional Education, we'll explore three major results of school getting in the way of education. For those primarily concerned with youth in postsecondary education, this chapter is a must. Then we'll step back in chapter 4, Reality Check: Insights from School Leaders, where I share what I learned from interviews with several local school leaders. Chapter 5, A New Paradigm for Education, lays the foundation for discussing the same.

The rest of the book explores each of the five features of the FACES framework. Chapter 6, Fun, breaks the mold of conventional education by discussing how enjoyment facilitates learning. Chapter 7, Affirmation, explains why it's important to validate the learner, making the chapter especially useful to advocates concerned about diversity, equity, and inclusion in education. Chapter 8, Challenge, emphasizes the power of positive relationships as well as rigor in youth development and dispels the practice of labeling youth. In chapter 9, Expression, we'll learn about autonomy and agency, akin to what educators call "voice and choice." The book then culminates with the indispensable chapter 10, Success. No advocate, especially those in higher education, can afford to miss this one, as it provides concrete steps that will greatly enhance the chances that youth will lead fulfilling and prosperous lives.

Introduction

My Journey

The experiences that inspired this new paradigm for education are both professional and deeply personal. My career as a teacher began as a substitute in the New York City public schools and ended as a university professor. By then, I had accumulated about eight years of experience teaching students from kindergarten to college. (Incidentally, during that time I had the opportunity to teach the daughter of President Biden, proof that as an educator, you never know who you might influence.) I was a highly intuitive educator, always looking for creative ways to intrinsically motivate students. To me, nothing was more rewarding than watching them grow. The awards and appreciation that I received from colleagues and students were affirming but secondary.

My career in education also includes various leadership roles. After teaching in New York, I was assistant director at the Clearinghouse on Urban Education, sponsored by the U.S. Department of Education. There I learned that ninth grade is when many students decide to drop out of school. Thus, the apathy I had observed among them as a substitute teacher was nothing unusual; it was part of a national phenomenon. Later, in New Orleans, I directed an alternative education program for high school dropouts in one role and then trained administrators and teachers throughout the state in another. More recently, before heading my own consulting firm, I worked in Virginia as a researcher in the central office at one of the nation's largest and most reputable school districts.

Even greater than my diverse skill set, the impacts of my

personal experiences have contributed to developing this new paradigm. Despite growing up in an impoverished community in New Orleans, I excelled in school. At age fifteen, I was awarded a scholarship by A Better Chance, Inc. (still in operation today) to attend a college preparatory school in the suburbs of Philadelphia. The environment sometimes felt like a foreign country. Overall, however, I enjoyed the experience tremendously and completed high school with academic distinction. Afterward, I attended Harvard University where my academic performance was lackluster. Finishing with a C-plus average, I might even go so far as to say that I graduated "*Thank ya, Lawdy!*"[9] Nonetheless, aside from their rich intellectual stimulation, both experiences made me aware of how social factors strongly influence the performance of youth.

Given my journey, I've experienced education from many diverse angles: as a student, educator, researcher, not to mention as a parent. So, my insights come from having been "to the mountaintop," studying at some of the nation's most reputable institutions, as well as from "around the block," experiencing diverse roles and settings.

How to Use This Book

Inspired by the courageous freedom fighter of the Underground Railroad in Lincoln's time, Harriet Tubman, this book is intended primarily for those whom I call Tubman Educators. These individuals often work outside of schools in community-based organizations that develop youth through after-school and other enrichment programs. Many, however, work within the regular school system and at any level, from teacher to superintendent. Despite the regulations that constrain schools, Tubman Educators go above, beneath, or around the conventional education system to foster the well-being of young learners. As mentors, they recognize, develop, and defend the need for emotional fulfillment. Above all, they are the individuals who refuse to let school get in the way of education and instead provide the support that youth truly need to succeed.

This book is also written as a guide for parents. The first teacher of every child is the parent. The book aims to expand your understanding of potential pitfalls within the current system and how to surmount them so that your child will flourish. With a clearer picture of the challenges confronting your child, you will be able to make better decisions as their advocate. The book may be especially valuable to parents who homeschool, or those concerned about: (1) their child's apathy or underachievement, (2) getting into the "right" school, or (3) transitioning from one school level to another (e.g., middle to high school or from high school to college).

This book may also aid university-level educators who are aware that their institutions not only inherit the problem of schooling but often exacerbate it. As counselors and mentors, they, too, circumvent the prevailing educational paradigm to make a pivotal difference in the lives of young people. The book may be especially valuable to those who prepare teachers and educational leaders as well as those involved in student career services, which I consider to be the Achilles heel of higher education.

Last, this book encourages policymakers, from local school boards to state legislators, to give greater weight to the nonacademic needs of young people when establishing the laws and regulations that shape our schools.

Finally, I offer two key tips to help all readers get the most out of this book. First and foremost, read this book intelligently—not intellectually. The intelligent reader will recognize that such phrases as "some teachers," "many parents," and "most students" do not mean all teachers, parents, and students. The intelligent reader recognizes and respects nuances. The intellectual reader, however, gets hopelessly bogged down in the quicksand of minutiae. Second, please understand that this call to youth advocacy is not an argument against academic rigor. That would be nonsensical. In and of itself, rigor is good; it encourages growth. Whether on the playing field with young athletes or inside the classroom with young scholars, rigorous training promotes the development of skill and thus performance. Like anything else, however, rigor must be pursued in proper proportion to derive its benefits. This book warns all not to pursue rigor at the expense of emotional well-being. For when that happens, performance can never be optimal.

This book is therefore dedicated to all young people so that they might flourish. It is written so that they might learn who they are, why they are here, and what they must do to succeed in school as well as in life. Ultimately, therefore, it is about far more than education—this book is about the spiritual well-being of our young people. For without the sense of purpose and joy that stem from emotional fulfillment, we are spiritually impaired. It is the development of that sense of direction and enthusiasm which, as we shall see, conventional schooling often impedes. With those ends in mind then, I invite you to join me in promoting a new and powerful paradigm for education. A paradigm that could transform the lives of youth:

Passion propels performance!

This new paradigm is rooted in the idea that school was made for our children; our children were not made for school. This paradigm embraces the belief that conventional education impedes the performance of youth, making them skillful but not willful. This new paradigm therefore demands that you—whether a youth development professional or schoolteacher, parent or principal, university administrator or school board member,

Don't let school get in the way of education!

Part I

CHAPTER 1

The Broccoli Model of Education

If achievement is imperative, then effort is essential; and if effort is essential, then motivation must be central. Conventional school is designed almost to suppress motivation.

—**Ted Kolderie, distinguished senior fellow, Center for Policy Design**

To fully appreciate why I call for a new paradigm for education, it is essential that you have a clear picture of the field's current circumstances. This chapter serves that purpose. Here, I expand on some of the core ideas presented in the book's introduction. We'll take it up a notch by delving into some critical statistics to provide a background for a few exemplary stories from youth themselves. Then, I present the perspectives of those who are recognized as experts in their fields. What you are about to hear aren't my words but theirs. Remember: The conditions are already there; they always have been. All I'm doing is connecting the dots to make this subtle picture clearer so that you can become a more effective youth advocate.

A host of national education reform initiatives and policies over the last several decades appear to have had little effect on student achievement in general.[1] Since the 1970s, results from the National Assessment of Educational Progress, often referred to as the Nation's Report Card, suggest that most kids are not fulfilling their potential academically.[2] For example, by the time they reach twelfth grade, fewer than two out of every five students (37 percent) read proficiently, and one in four (24 percent) reasons proficiently in mathematics[3] (see Figure 1).

Now pause for a second and think of all the technological progress we have made over the same period, the last fifty years or so. Look at your cell phone for a moment as an example. Mind-boggling, isn't it?

This educational inertia begins to make perfect sense, however, once you factor in an important feature that characterizes most reform initiatives, including the current one, the Common Core State Standards. These reforms give little attention to an essential ingredient necessary for improving human performance: motivation. Instead, they call for students to upgrade their knowledge and skills and require that teachers do the same. One initiative after another, policymakers continue to align education with *standards* but not with *students*. Yes, education reform initiatives have raised the bar for student performance without considering the most fundamental resource needed to achieve it. This emphasis on standards and rigor with little regard for the role of human emotion in teaching and learning is what I refer to as the Broccoli Model of Education.[4]

Grade 12 **Mathematics**
Forty Percent below NAEP Basic

YEAR	Below NAEP Basic	NAEP Basic	NAEP Proficient	NAEP Advanced	At or above NAEP Proficient
2019	40	35	21	3	24
2015	38*	37*	22	3	25
2005	39	38*	21	2*	23

Grade 12 **Reading**
Thirty Percent below NAEP Basic

YEAR	Below NAEP Basic	NAEP Basic	NAEP Proficient	NAEP Advanced	At or above NAEP Proficient
2019	30	33	31	6	37
2015	28*	35*	31	6	37
1992[1]	20*	39*	36*	4*	40*

* Significantly different p<.05 from 2019
[1] Accommodations not permitted.

Figure 1. NAEP 2019 Mathematics and Reading Achievement Levels of Students in Twelfth Grade.

In my workshops with live audiences around the United States and abroad, people agree that broccoli and soymilk are awesome examples of highly nutritious foods. Yet, nearly every participant in the audience also agrees that, despite their nutritional value, the two are not a combination they would enjoy eating. Why? "Because it smells absolutely horrible and probably tastes the same!" is a typical response from workshop participants. To illustrate the point, I've actually showcased a bowl of raw broccoli doused with soymilk (see Figure 2).

Figure 2. A Still from Facing the Broccoli Model of Education.

Decade after decade, adults have been asking—no, not asking but demanding—kids to consume educational standards that are highly nutritious, so to speak, but in a form far too unpalatable emotionally. Usually, standards consist of rote memorization of facts, lectures, and assignments without a clear connection to real life. Let me give you a concrete example.

Once, while visiting a local high school, I observed a principal putting a student on the spot in a Spanish language class by asking him to stand and conjugate a verb. Such academic emphasis on grammatical structure—*rather than actual use of the language*—is why many of us are incapable of speaking a second language even after years of study. Would it not have been much more useful to have demanded instead that the student said something practical in Spanish? If not a brief conversation, then maybe just a meaningful sentence or two? And, with all due respect, having walked the streets of Madrid and Montevideo, Salamanca and Santo Domingo, Guadalajara, Panama City, and Buenos Aires, I can confirm personally that a more practical approach to teaching Spanish and other languages would be more effective than the emphasis that many teachers place on grammar.

Now, don't get me wrong. My purpose here is not to insult educators or belittle the hard work that so many of them do. Having been a teacher myself, I hold a great deal of admiration and respect for the women and men doing the invaluable job of developing our youth in schools each day. Unfortunately, however, many educators are bound or blinded by the status quo. I'd even go so far as to say that many educators are themselves held hostage by an educational system insensitive to the emotional needs of students as well as their own. Consequently, many teachers find it difficult to do little more than follow their marching orders as issued by the state, or in the case of private schools, the administration.

I must reiterate that my intent is merely to connect the dots about what we know is and has been going on in education for decades so that you make an informed decision about your child's future. My aim is to help you and other youth advocates recognize, develop, and defend the need for emotional fulfillment in school. You see, the Broccoli Model of Education by design focuses on your child's intellectual development at the expense of their emotional development. And you need to know that the implications of this approach to education are costly, sometimes even tragic.

But you need not rely on my word or experience alone to validate this assertion. Take a look at what national research from three independent sources tells us about how youth in general are experiencing school today:

- Results from the High School Survey of Student Engagement tell us that students are bored in school not only because the material is not interesting (81 percent) or personally relevant (42 percent) but also because of a lack of interaction with their teachers (35 percent).[5]

- In a 2016 Gallup survey among roughly one million students attending public and private schools across the fifty states, engagement (defined as "involvement in and enthusiasm for school") fell from nearly 75 percent of students in the fifth grade to a low of about 32 percent of students by eleventh grade. (See Figure 3.)[6]

- In a survey conducted by the U.S. Department of Education (see Figure 4), when asked "What is your favorite subject?" the number one answer among ninth graders at public and private schools nationwide was "physical education." And when asked precisely the opposite, their least favorite subject was . . . you guessed it—math.[7] Combined, these two responses clearly suggest that the kids are fed up with the Broccoli Model.

The Broccoli Model of Education

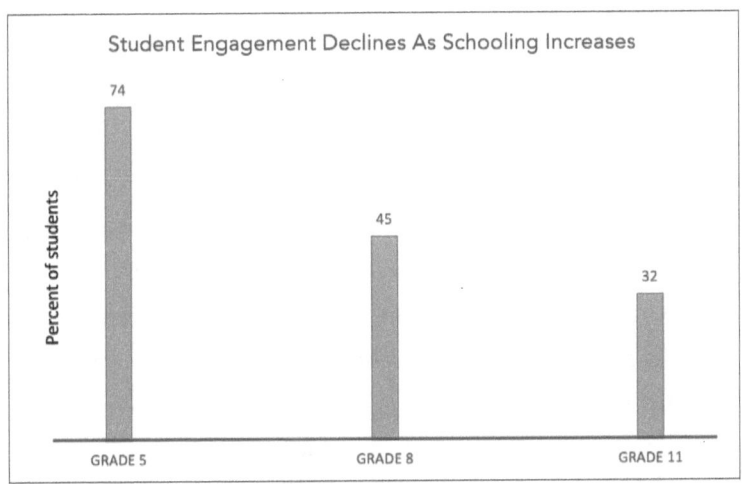

Figure 3. Source: 2016 Gallup Student Poll.

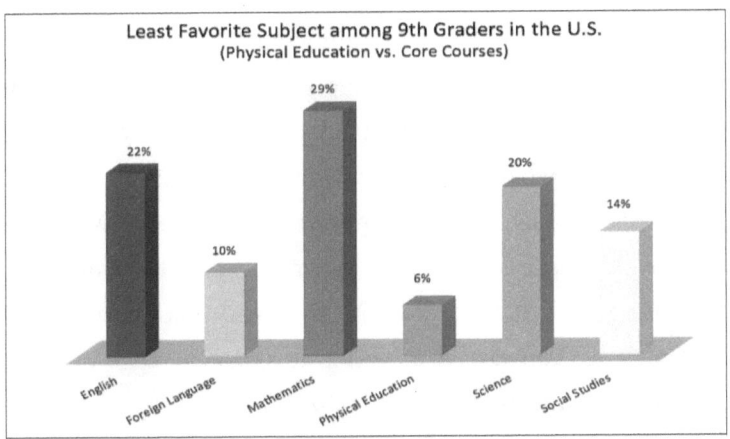

Figure 4. Source: National Center for Education Statistics (2011). High School Longitudinal Survey 2009.

Now, if you're like many adults, your first impulse might be to dismiss all this with remarks like, "Well, whadaya expect, they're kids!" In fact, this typical reaction reminds me of not one but two encounters I've had with educators in recent years. The first took place while I was conducting a seminar on the topic of student engagement for about thirty-five teacher leaders in training to become school principals. "I'm sick and tired of students criticizing my teaching!" exclaimed one of the trainees. "They're not even qualified to evaluate my instruction." Now, just apply this scenario to some other field, let's say, technology. Although you as a consumer may have little or none of the technical knowledge required to build a computer, should the engineer who does value your opinion as a user? Can you see the flawed reasoning in the educator's perspective?

In the second encounter, while discussing the climate at a local charter school, one administrator indicated they had conducted an engagement survey in-house and learned that their students were "just about as disengaged as everywhere else." But then when I asked, "So what have you done with that information? How did you respond?" She replied, "Well, you see, the kids just need to buckle down . . ." In other words, the only thing the educator did with that information was make light of it. In contrast, dear youth advocate, I suggest to you that until we adults are willing to buckle up with a new paradigm for education, our children will continue to suffer. Yes, my friend, the Broccoli Model of Education is alive and well.

One way in which I find this approach to education particularly disturbing is how some schools respond—or fail to respond—to the issue of bullying. It astounds me to read about parents winning millions of dollars in lawsuits because a school

The Broccoli Model of Education

did little or nothing about bullying. The inadequate response from schools to this problem makes crystal clear the emphasis that the Broccoli Model places on the acquisition of academic knowledge and skills to the exclusion of students' emotional well-being.

I doubt that anyone needs a degree in psychology to understand that a child, or an adult for that matter, is far less likely to learn or perform well when they are constantly being molested. If you are the target of sexual harassment in the workplace, you are bound to feel stressed and uncomfortable, to say the least. Should it surprise anyone that such an emotional state diminishes one's performance? Well, the same applies to our children when someone is harassing them at school. Bullying, as we know, is associated with a host of negative emotional and psychological effects.[8]

Unfortunately, I have heard educators comment, for example, "Kids are kids and are going to be mean to each other sometimes. But I can't do anything about that. I'm just here to teach." While I fully agree with the first statement, I couldn't disagree more with the remaining. Bullying should not be viewed merely as the concern of individual students but as the collective responsibility of the adults in the school to maintain order. Just as a supervisor in the workplace should be obligated to ensure a work environment conducive to productivity, so should the educators at school take responsibility for creating and maintaining a social climate conducive to learning. The belief that educators should focus on instruction without prioritizing the emotional well-being of students undermines the very learning that schools seek to promote. Ignoring social conflict in the classroom is just as bad as ignoring sexual harassment in the workplace. Thus, the academic focus of schooling without adequate attention to students' emotional well-being can cause educators to ignore or even create an inhospitable environment for learning. And when that happens, then school is getting in the way of education.

Due to its neglect of students' emotional needs, the Broccoli Model of Education breeds alienation from school as well as anxiety among youth. Perhaps nothing will impress upon you the degree to which they experience anguish and frustration toward the educational system as much as testimonies from youth themselves. To appreciate the truth of this, I urge you to familiarize yourself with three videos on YouTube by youth who have fervently expressed their sentiments about conventional schooling.

Experiences of Actual Students

One video features an actual classroom experience of Jeff Bliss, a high school student in Texas, secretly captured in class on the cell phone of a fellow student. Frustrated by the lack of engaging instructional methods, Bliss launches a tirade against his teacher before she ejects him from class. Ironically, as he races to the front of the classroom in anger, he passes a student apparently sleeping on the desk right in front of the teacher, thus validating Bliss's outrage. The incident later becomes a topic on local news in which Bliss, who also had previously

The Broccoli Model of Education

dropped out of school, expressed no regret for his defiance but better yet declared, "It needed to be said!"[9]

Next, see the video produced by Darryll S. Amoako of England, known as Suli Breaks. His video, aptly entitled, *Why I Hate School But Love Education*, says it all with more than 9.5 million views. Delivered in his unique style of poetry and urban rap, Suli has become an international sensation. Check out this small clip from his lyrics highlighting the difference between education and school:

> All I'm saying is that, if there was a family tree
> hard work and education would be related,
> but school would probably be a distant cousin.
> Because if education is the key, school is the lock.
> Because it rarely ever develops your mind
> to the point where it can perceive red as green
> and continue to go when someone else said stop.
> Because as long as you follow the rules and pass the exams, you're cool . . . [10]

A third powerful and provocative video, "I Sued the School System," by Richard Williams, known as "Prince Ea," garnered eight million views in just about a year in 2016. (But that's small potatoes compared to his one billion views on Facebook!)[11] Beyond the age of youth and with a degree in anthropology, this young man illustrates the same point as the others using a combination of drama and rap. He plays the role of an attorney in court before judge and jury, charging modern schooling with "killing creativity, individuality, and being intellectually abusive. He's [School's] an ancient institution that has outlived his usage."[12]

But if listening to the passionate pleas and opinions of youth hasn't convinced you that the Broccoli Model of Education is real, then perhaps it's time to examine what those generally considered as experts have to say on the subject. After looking at a few recent examples, it should be clear that the complaints of youth about schooling are not merely the ordinary whining of kids; they are the sincere cries of young souls yearning for liberation and expression as suggested here:

> *I hate school because I love learning. All they ever want is work. They don't care if you learn . . . Just get good grades and make the school look good.*[13]

What Researchers Have to Say

Who would believe that one of the most popular TED Talks in the world (roughly seventy-eight million views as of this writing) suggests that school actually undermines education? Just go online and see for yourself how Sir Ken Robinson, reminiscent of the dorky college professor, offers a lecture as humorous as it is insightful about our public educational system, entitled, "Do Schools Kill Creativity?" He explains as follows:

> What we do know is, if you're not prepared to be wrong, you'll never come up with anything

original . . . And by the time they get to be adults, most kids have lost that capacity. They have become frightened of being wrong . . . And we're now running national education systems where mistakes are the worst thing you can make. And the result is that we are educating people out of their creative capacities . . . I believe this passionately, that we don't grow into creativity, we grow out of it. Or rather, we get educated out of it.[14]

Perhaps no one in recent times has spoken more harshly about our educational system than authors Tony Wagner and Ted Dintersmith. Wagner currently serves as a senior research fellow at the National Learning Policy Institute after several positions at Harvard University, where he received his master's and doctorate degrees in education. Dintersmith is an accomplished venture capitalist and an education philanthropist, equally as passionate as Wagner about education reform. Let's see how they translate the sentiments of Jeff Bliss, Suli Breaks, and Prince Ea in their provocative book, *Most Likely to Succeed: Preparing Our Kids for the Innovation Era*. Note that the authors speak to the fact that the concern about the process of schooling is *not* one confronting just children from families with limited means socially and economically: "The crisis is ubiquitous. Every child in America is at risk."[15]

Today, our education system has become the American Nightmare. It saps the joy of learning from every child and teacher. Classrooms jump through endless hoops that have nothing to do with life skills. Our education policy-makers lack vision and perspective, and prioritize the need for an outdated version of "accountability," not the long-term interests of our children. For millions of young Americans, school is where their hopes for a meaningful life die, instead of spring into life.[16]

In short, many of our most progressive thinkers are in concert with our youth in asserting that schooling often undermines rather than inspires academic achievement. What irony! Not only are these voices saying that schooling stifles creativity but also that it does so at a time when the ability to think creatively is critical for competitiveness in the marketplace, not to mention fulfillment in life. Decades ago, Albert Einstein alluded to the same in declaring, "Imagination is more important than intelligence."[17]

In sum, today's educational system is like a train out of control, running full speed ahead, driven by policies and practices that threaten the emotional wellness of youth. Many continue to discard this line of thinking as though it were nothing other than a concern among the unmotivated. But the accounts reviewed here span youth from all backgrounds and persuasions. These accounts reflect the need for an entirely different paradigm or model of education, one based on principles of human motivation and not merely cognitive development.

The Broccoli Model of Education

The Broccoli Model is, in my opinion, an artifact of the industrial age. Beware therefore of applying a business model to education. That model, governed by efficiency, operates on the basis of a widget as its unit of production. Your child is not a widget. And education is a human process that can no longer tolerate the efficient, assembly-line model of production. If you don't heed this warning, schooling may literally run over your child, causing an accident from which they might never recover.

To come full circle, what you need to understand as a youth advocate is that there's a quiet war going on in the field of education. A battle fought between an insensitive system, on the one hand, and advocates for change, on the other hand. And what's at stake? Why, nothing less than the hearts, minds, and souls of our children. I submit to you as an advocate, therefore, that rather than waiting on children to *buckle down*, what we as enlightened adults need to do is *buckle up*! In other words, let's take responsibility and action capable of producing different results from what we've been getting now for decades. In addition to setting high educational standards and rigorous coursework, let's value what children are saying about their educational experiences in order to produce a "new and improved" version of school. Let's challenge rather than conform to the belief that cognitive development without emotional wellness is simply "the way it is." Let's advocate together for a new educational order.

In summary, let's be clear about the status of education as far as students are concerned. In general, a wide gap exists between the perspectives of youth and how adults feel about schooling. The gap is particularly troubling, because although students are in fact the primary customers of schools, their opinions and satisfaction don't seem to mean a whole lot to many adults. Instead, the latter often expect that children will eat their vegetables, so to speak, because they are good for them, never mind their taste or lack thereof. This is the essence of the Broccoli Model of Education. Indeed, the holy grail of education as we know it today consists of high academic standards backed by rigorous coursework.

But what if, as a result of the lack of emotional fulfillment that many youth experience in education, they actually end up increasing their chances of failing rather than succeeding in school, not to mention in life itself? In the next chapter, we'll consider such a possibility by examining the tragic outcome of one adolescent whose educational experience serves as a quintessential example of how the Broccoli Model can lead youth astray.

AUTHOR'S KEY POINTS

1. The current emphasis in schools on standards and rigor with little or no regard for emotional fulfillment among students is what I call the "Broccoli Model of Education."
2. In general, the further students advance through school, the less engaged they become.
3. Students themselves as well as educational experts express great concern about the disconnect between the needs of youth and the process of schooling.

MY KEY REFLECTIONS

1. What in this chapter left the biggest impression on me?

2. What personal experiences, if any, did this chapter bring to mind?

3. What action might I or others take based on what I've learned?

CHAPTER 2

Education Dilemma: Academic Rigor versus Emotional Well-Being

One does not become enlightened by imagining figures of light, but by making the darkness conscious. The latter procedure, however, is disagreeable and therefore not popular.

—Carl Jung, Swiss psychologist and psychiatrist

Decades after the Civil Rights Movement, the United States continues to struggle with issues related to its social diversity. Demographic projections suggest that this diversity and its complexity will only increase as the twenty-first century progresses. Prior to 1970, for example, about one out of every eight Americans was non-White; by 2060 the proportion is expected to increase substantially to about one out of every three.[1] And, as of this writing, roughly 80 percent of teachers are White while a majority of the nearly fifty million students enrolled in public schools are non-Hispanic Whites or "People of Color."[2] Significant shifts in population, therefore, will continue to bring issues known as "diversity, equity, and inclusion" (DEI) to the forefront of national conversations. One major outcome of those conversations has been the attention given to systemic racism.

Recognition of racism's systemic nature has led to calls for change at an institutional as well as individual level. If the nation is to realize its egalitarian ideals, then all systems, from health to criminal justice, from government to private industry, and yes—education, too—must answer the call. Until education leaders can recognize the need for reform in their own institutions and then take appropriate action, their schools may inadvertently perpetuate systemic racism, which some have referred to as the "other pandemic."

Addressing the concern about institutional racism, in my opinion, expands the opportunity for schools to support the well-being of all students, regardless of their ethnicity. School leaders, for example, might ask themselves the following questions: How can schools foster better connection and engagement? How might they reduce anxiety, stress, and depression among students and teachers? Last, how can schools promote social equity rather than social injustice?

To explore these questions, this chapter reviews a tragic

story that culminated with the death of an honor student decades ago. That story was revealed in Robert Anson's book, *Best Intentions: The Education and Killing of Edmund Perry*. As an alumnus of the very same scholarship program that hosted the book's central character, I find the story particularly poignant. Moreover, I believe it demonstrates that answers to many of the concerns triggered by the growing diversity in American schools can be found in three sources: school culture, climate, and leadership. And because I believe that this tragedy could have happened almost anywhere in America, the name of Perry's school need not be mentioned. Let us look to the past, then, to enlighten a path for the future of our youth.

Shadows That Shatter

At the twinkly-eyed age of thirteen, Edmund Perry had achieved something special. Despite growing up in the impoverished community of Harlem, New York, he had earned a scholarship to a prestigious school in New England. "Eddie" was full of excitement—and no doubt fear. After all, leaving Harlem at such a young age for "ABC Academy" (a pseudonym) must have felt like leaving the comfort of Earth's familiar atmosphere and heading straight for the moon. But for a better chance at an excellent education, this voyage was worth risking the unknown. By age seventeen, however, something had changed—dramatically. The honor student's enthusiasm had been replaced by anger and depression.

Moreover, no one would have imagined that just ten days after graduation, young Perry would be dead.

The circumstances surrounding Perry's passing were controversial. Members of his community saw his death at the hand of a White undercover police officer as unjust and racially motivated. Nevertheless, a jury concluded that the officer acted justifiably in self-defense during an alleged assault by Perry. This writing does not concern his guilt or innocence. Rather, it discusses Anson's well-researched findings, which I contend show how school culture and climate can harm students.

Just three years prior to Perry's death, faculty members at the Academy produced a study of Black dropouts at the school, which concluded that "the vast majority had done so not for academic or disciplinary reasons, but because, as one of the study's authors put it, 'they had been psychologically crushed.'"[3] It is easy then to understand how Perry could have experienced depression and engaged increasingly in risky behaviors that may even have cost him his life.

Moreover, Anson also brought to light that indulgence in risky behaviors was commonplace for a substantial portion of the school's predominantly White and wealthy student body. Drug use was considered both "an exclusively white phenomenon" and a persistent problem at the Academy. Teachers offered various explanations. One, with considerable experience in drug counseling, is quoted as saying, "This can be a cold, hard place . . . you don't have to think too hard to imagine how seductive drugs can be."[4]

So how might this school have unwittingly harmed the

well-being of its students? And how might schools today avoid repeating those mistakes? To answer these questions, education leaders must be willing to venture out of their comfort zones. A willingness to open the door to such conversations is the first step toward identifying root causes. Let us do so by discussing culture, climate, and leadership.

Understanding School Culture and Climate

How could a school's environment possibly undermine the psychological wellness of adolescents? Let's first distinguish between two pertinent and related terms frequently used interchangeably: school culture and climate.

According to *Merriam-Webster*, culture is "a set of shared attitudes, values, goals, and practices that characterize an organization."[5] It encompasses both visible and invisible elements that give an organization its unique identity. Culture is about how we do things (practices) based on the dominant beliefs, values, and attitudes we hold as a group. In contrast, the same source defines climate as "the prevailing influence or environmental conditions characterizing a group or period."[6] The word "atmosphere" then follows as a synonym. Climate is thus the social atmosphere that we experience as a by-product of our interactions with culture. School climate is therefore feedback. It tells *how well* the culture is working and *for whom*. In short, culture is an institution's social road map, while climate is how stakeholders feel about the journey itself.

School Culture and Student Well-Being

As long as educators view their primary mission as equipping youth with academic skills and give inadequate attention to emotional development, they are likely to overlook how their school cultures and climates might compromise students' well-being. As an example, consider the response from faculty at ABC Academy in reaction to the study of Black dropouts. Anson writes: "More than most schools, ABC Academy prided itself on tradition, on 'its way of doing things' . . . But when the study was presented . . . with recommendations for changes, the reaction was indifference . . . 'What do you expect with kids from this background? . . . We shouldn't really expect a higher level of success . . . It's sink or swim. If they make it, fine. If they don't, so be it.'"[7]

Thus, highly focused on academic rigor, the school's culture fostered a climate of indifference to students' emotional well-being. Evidence, as we shall see, suggests that this problem is prevalent today. What education needs therefore is a cultural shift—one that elevates emotional development *above* that of cognitive skills.

Consider this definition of trauma from the Substance Abuse and Mental Health Services Administration:

> Individual trauma results from an event, series of events, or set of circumstances that is experienced by an individual as physically or emotionally harmful or life threatening and that has lasting adverse effects on the individual's functioning

and mental, physical, social, emotional, or spiritual well-being.[8]

This broad definition seems particularly relevant to students at private boarding schools, who are removed from the emotional supports of home. Edmund Perry and so many of his peers at ABC Academy were arguably traumatized due to persistent exposure to an educational experience that repeatedly injured them emotionally and spiritually. In the case of Black students, racism was indeed a factor afflicting their emotional development. However, it was by no means the only factor. An even greater cause, in my humble opinion, was an educational paradigm that espouses the notion that acquiring academic skills is the key purpose of schooling. This paradigm persists with serious implications for students today.

Rigor versus Well-Being

Because educators continue to embrace a fundamental value that assaulted Perry and so many of his peers, his tragedy remains relevant to education today. That fundamental value and key feature of American education is *the pursuit of academic rigor at the expense of emotional well-being*. Underlying this feature are two main drivers of educational policy and practice today. First and foremost, as previously mentioned, is the notion or paradigm that intelligence is the major factor in human achievement. Second, the needs of industry (e.g., science, technology, engineering, and mathematics) also exert tremendous influence on the educational system. Combined, these two forces encourage schools in general, whether public or private, to operate on a business model that views young minds as raw materials to be cultivated for economic ends. Accordingly, we exchange educational effectiveness for instructional efficiency; we demand that students spend years studying academic subjects, some of which they may never use. And in the process, they learn little about themselves as the engine of achievement. Thus, we make youth skillful but not willful.

In contrast to the paradigm underlying the current educational system, there is the notion that emotion, rather than intelligence, constitutes the foundation of human achievement. To understand how and why this might be so, allow me to briefly introduce the self-determination theory of motivation (SDT), developed by Edward L. Deci and Richard M. Ryan. Self-determination asserts that there are three psychological needs fundamental to wellness and optimal performance in any endeavor: autonomy, competence, and relatedness.[9] To the extent that schools support these needs, students may flourish. Likewise, to the extent that they obstruct these needs, students may flounder. Unfortunately, much of what we observe in the educational system suggests that the latter occurs all too often.

Instead of promoting autonomy, schools instill compliance, as was highlighted by *Harvard Magazine* in a 2019 study titled "Rigor with Joy? Rethinking the American High School." In that work, researchers described education nationwide as a climate of "bored, disengaged compliance."[10]

Education Dilemma: Academic Rigor versus Emotional Well-Being

Many students never experience a true sense of competence through schooling arguably because of its irrelevance to real life. And because engagement declines as students move further along the educational pipeline, they naturally become increasingly less likely to achieve a true sense of competence.

As for relatedness, school leaders should be particularly mindful of this factor, given the mental health crisis currently afflicting the nation's youth. No school administrator can afford to disregard the need for relatedness among all students, regardless of race/ethnicity, in light of the following:

- Among adolescents aged twelve to seventeen, one out of every four have experienced either a substance use disorder or a major depressive episode.[11]

- Suicide ranks as the second leading cause of death among youth between ten to fourteen years of age and the third among those aged fifteen to twenty-four.[12]

- A majority of teens worry about a shooting happening at their school, as mass shootings in American society are now commonplace.[13]

In conclusion, the tension between academic rigor and emotional well-being that existed in Perry's day as well as now stems from the way we see and do the business of education. Our current paradigm places rigor and well-being at odds when in fact they should be complementary. Thus, the traumatic experiences of youth at ABC Academy, although decades ago, still serve as a warning to all today: *Academic rigor at the expense of emotional well-being is not only misguided but dangerous!*

Bias Breeds Blindness

If the cultures and climates of our schools operate in the interests of industry more than that of students, what can be done about it? What strategic moves might be made in this moment of opportunity spawned by today's two-pronged crisis? Leadership. Organizations and systems are shaped by leaders. A major challenge in effective leadership, however, involves the biases of leadership itself. These biases are naturally influenced by the leader's cultural background (hence the term "cultural bias").

With culture as the lens through which we perceive reality, we act in and on the world accordingly. Each of us acts, usually unconsciously, in ways consistent with our views, beliefs, and values. This is true whether one heads the White House or the schoolhouse. Bias itself is not inherently bad; it is necessary. It is part of the cultural map we need in order to interpret reality. The problem comes when we are *unaware* of our biases. When this happens, our actions can have unintended consequences that negatively impact an entire community.

It is essential therefore that school leaders be aware of their own cultural biases. Such awareness is a major step toward enabling them to create a supportive climate for all. But when unchecked, bias can lead to blindness. Consequently, a school leader's inability to see and understand the perspectives of other stakeholders—especially students—can ultimately harm them, the leader, and the school itself.

Let There Be Light

Ironically, Edmund Perry's story takes place in the name of educational opportunity. Certainly, we can and must do better for our youth. In addition to giving students a better chance, we must show them a better way—to learn, to live, to thrive. What can education leaders do to reduce the likelihood that schooling will stifle rather than support the development of young people? How can leaders obliterate the shadows of compliance, disengagement, and racism that shatter students' wellness?

Leaders must take action to cultivate supportive learning environments. First, they must engage in self-reflection and be open to feedback from others regarding their own beliefs and biases. Here they must be willing to risk feeling uncomfortable. Psychologist Carl Jung asserted our reluctance to accept or even acknowledge the "darker side" of ourselves.[14] We often feel better about ourselves, he contended, when we project our deficiencies on others. But in the case of schooling, do we not as adults and administrators have an obligation to prioritize the welfare of our students'?

School leaders and teachers then need to discuss their beliefs about the goals and methods of education. They should identify potential threats in their school cultures to students' well-being by assessing their climates. To facilitate both, school leaders should also seek input from students and parents. In this way, leaders will inspire trust and thus strengthen their efforts to build more supportive learning environments. Such collaboration, when authentic, has the potential to truly transform an organization.

As a result of these steps, students will enjoy greater engagement and less distress. Teachers as well as parents will express greater satisfaction. And in time, the reputation of the institution itself will flourish.

The great irony of Perry's story is that ABC Academy was built on the idea of well-being *and* rigor. Established in 1781 upon Puritan values, the school apparently strayed from the credo proclaimed by its founder and retold by Anson (italics are his):

> It is expected that the attention of instructors to the *disposition* of the minds and morals of the youth under their charge will *exceed every other care*; well considering that though goodness without knowledge is weak and feeble, yet knowledge without goodness is dangerous, and that both united form the noblest character, and lay the surest foundation of usefulness to mankind.[15]

The challenge confronting educators therefore is not an "either-or" proposition. It is about promoting both wellness and rigor. That being said, let's be clear about our priorities.

The need for spiritual and emotional well-being was affirmed with eloquent simplicity much further back, in the time of Jesus: "For what shall it profit a man, if he shall gain the whole world, and lose his own soul?"[16] The tragic story of Edmund Perry reminds us of the answer.

In the introduction, I described my leaving home in New Orleans to attend a prep school in suburban Pennsylvania as a journey to the moon. Like young Perry, I too had ventured far beyond my personal comfort zone as an adolescent in pursuit of educational opportunity. Compared to his experience, however, I surmise that mine was much more fulfilling emotionally. But why?

To answer this question, I share some of my own story here and later in the book. I hope that doing so will also give you a sense of the challenges that likely confronted him and others who may attend school under similar circumstances.

Like most large cities, New Orleans, then as now, had more than its share of poverty, crime, and deprivation. As a young child, I was unaware of the extent of these conditions all around me. By the time I reached junior high school, however, that began to change.

Because we received government assistance in the form of food stamps as well as public housing, I can remember feeling embarrassed at times when some of my peers would look down on me, making disparaging remarks. One girl that I liked, for example, told me that her mother would not approve of me because "boys who live in the [city's housing] projects only want one thing." And later on, when I was old enough to work part-time as a busboy and waiter in the fancy hotels downtown, it was hard to get a cab ride home at times after finishing the night shift. As soon as I would tell a driver my address, they would often say something like, "I'm sorry, my man, but I can't go there . . . it's too dangerous." My academic scholarship therefore transported me to a place that was unlike my home in some very fundamental ways.

The physical environment of this quaint, suburban town, Swarthmore, was so beautiful that I often felt like Alice in Wonderland. During the fall as well as the spring seasons, the trees adorned themselves with leaves so diverse in shapes and colors that, for me, their splendor evoked visions of Mardi Gras. And for the first time in my life, I not only beheld the awesome beauty of snow-filled landscapes but got to play in them as well!

As for the social environment, though alien, it was hardly alienating. I lived in a house renovated and supported by the community with eight other boys, two tutors from the prestigious college nearby, and our resident directors, and a White married couple. As you might imagine, this man and his wife were not ordinary people. I mean, how many people in America would take on a job of not only supervising but also living with nine teenage boys despite the racial gap between them? Together, we lived as a pretty cohesive family, thanks to their leadership.

The "ABC House" in Swarthmore, Pennsylvania, 1975.

The "ABC House" in Swarthmore, Pennsylvania, 2025.

A winter view from my bedroom window at the "ABC House" in Swarthmore.

A beautiful spring day in Swarthmore.

Education Dilemma: Academic Rigor versus Emotional Well-Being

At school, there was an intense and healthy curiosity between us and our peers. The nine in my cohort had hometowns spanning the country east of the Mississippi River. The boys from New York never ceased to astound the locals (as well as our cohort) with their tales of life in "The City." However, although from different parts of the country, our cohort was quite similar in background and culture. Three boys were Southerners, three from the Midwest, and three were Northeasterners who all spoke Spanish at home. Two of them became my best friends. Up until that time, I had no idea what a "Puerto Rican" was. These friends were thus my introduction to Latin American cultures.

Importantly, the local college community was also a huge bonus in my scholarship experience. Each year or so, the resident directors would select two students from there to serve as our tutors. These relationships also expanded our access to the college's resources, especially the gym. In addition, one of the community's most avid supporters of our program, Ann Geer, worked there. The most generous person I have ever known, she opened the door for me to become a member of the college's gospel choir. In fact, by the time of my senior year, one male student at the college facetiously suggested banning us from campus to reduce competition for the female coeds. (I confess, I was one of the offenders.)

Where I did experience some degree of alienation was in the local community and the high school. This was offset, however, by the fact that the community as a whole had assumed responsibility for establishing and maintaining the national scholarship program locally. On Sundays, for example, each

Don't Let School Get in the Way of Education

ABC student would spend the afternoon with a host family, giving the resident directors a much-needed break. This feature of the program deepened our connection to the community tremendously. For me, the kindness, generosity, and affluence of this White, Anglo-Saxon, Protestant community was absolutely astounding. Like Christopher Columbus, I had encountered what *for me* was indeed a new world.

Every day, reminders of how different life was there compared to my hometown were constant. And, for the most part, they were benign. At home, for example, with seven children including four teenage boys, my mother had to ration bread and milk to make ends meet. (If you're familiar with the appetite of just one teenage boy, then you know what I'm talking about.) Now, despite living with eight teenage boys, there were no limitations on food. I can still remember the delight I felt

Me, the author, at age fifteen, doubling up on breakfast—finally because I could.

one morning, checking with the resident directors about what I could have for breakfast. "You mean I can eat as much as I want?" "As much as you want," they cheerfully replied.

On the other hand, there were times when the sting of cultural alienation was uncomfortable or even painful. If you have ever traveled abroad, then you probably know that living in another culture can be downright disorienting. The effects can be particularly stressful when one's stay is lengthy and when the local language is not your own. And, whereas one might expect to encounter alienation abroad, experiencing it in one's own country can be unsettling, to say the least. I can remember, for instance, feeling odd when, on account of my New Orleans accent, a classmate sarcastically asked me to "speak English." On another occasion, it was my English teacher who embarrassed me in class by mocking my improper speech.

But however idyllic it might have been, the town was still part of the larger national culture. One day at school, my class was playing baseball during PE. As the catcher behind home plate, I observed a couple of local boys jesting in the direction of my "ABC buddy," Enrique, who was too far afield to hear anything. "C'mon, pick up the ball, Spic!" said one boy; the other laughed in response. Meanwhile, I just stood by, lost in curiosity. After school, seeking to understand the term I had no reference for, I asked Enrique what it meant. "That's what they call Puerto Ricans," he exclaimed angrily. "And if you ever say it again, I'm gonna punch you in the mouth!" Of course, once I explained to him how I heard the word at school, his anger toward me faded.

Later, as I continued to reflect on the situation, I asked myself: *So what must they be calling* me *when I'm in the outfield?*

Along the same lines, mentions of African or Latin Americans in the curriculum at school were either none or negative. And what we think of today as diversity among the faculty was nonexistent. Offsetting this situation, however, was the powerful influence of our resident directors, one of which was an unorthodox Catholic priest who, among other things, had marched with Dr. King during the Civil Rights Movement. Unsurprisingly yet ironically, they were the people who encouraged me to read the provocative book, *The Autobiography of Malcolm X*. Between their compassion for others and zeal for social justice, there was always room to talk about whatever was going on at school, at home, and in the world. And all did so each night when the thirteen of us managed to squeeze in around the great oval dinner table.

And like young Perry, I suspect that one of the most difficult challenges we all faced was that of adapting to the two disparate worlds we now had to navigate. The Christmas holidays weren't long enough in general to cause a problem. Spending the summer months "back in the hood," however, always made me wonder whether I was changing somehow as a result of my scholarship experience. Such a challenge, in my opinion, is beyond the capabilities of many if not most adolescents to resolve alone.

All in all, despite the difficulties I encountered, my high school experience overall was exciting and enjoyable. Moreover, it proved to be an excellent environment that enabled me and "my brothers" to excel academically. We all graduated on time and gained admission to top colleges as expected. Aside from our individual efforts, of course, I attribute such positive outcomes to the supportive social environment at home, the school, and in the community. Regardless of the challenges surrounding us, the ABC House was our safe haven. Through our peers, tutors, and resident directors, we received personal support and validation.

So, although I identified with many of the fundamental challenges that Edmund Perry experienced, I would venture to say the safe haven I enjoyed was something he lacked. Nonetheless, my time of trials and tribulations was yet to come. I'll share more about that in the pages ahead.

AUTHOR'S KEY POINTS

1. The current emphasis in schools on academic rigor with little or no regard for emotional fulfillment among youth is not only misguided but also dangerous.

2. Educators and advocates must prioritize the emotional development of youth.

3. Leaders of schools and educational programs must take concrete action to become aware of how their own institutions might undermine the emotional well-being of students.

MY KEY REFLECTIONS

1. What in this chapter left the biggest impression on me?

2. What personal experiences, if any, did this chapter bring to mind?

3. What action might I or others take based on what I've learned?

CHAPTER 3

Common Core Consequences of Conventional Education

The foundation of every state is the education of its youth.
—Diogenes, Greek philosopher

The tragic story in the previous chapter is extremely unusual, a worst-case scenario of how conventional education might cause youth to lose their way. In this chapter, however, we will see that the consequences of the Broccoli Model discussed in chapter 1 are not only commonplace but also far-reaching. Its effects go beyond alienation from school, impacting millions of lives and costing the economy trillions of dollars. In 2023 alone, only 33 percent of U.S. workers were engaged in their jobs, amounting to a loss in productivity of $1.9 trillion.[1] Therefore, as the Greek philosopher Diogenes espoused more than two thousand years ago, if you want to ensure the well-being of the nation, then prioritize the education of youth.

Let's consider some major consequences of conventional education by examining its effects in three areas: college, career, and citizenship. It is a given that not everyone needs a college degree to be successful. Attending college is therefore the least important of these three. Higher education remains, however, a key step for many in the pursuit of a satisfying career and life. Moreover, those who attend college achieve significantly better employment outcomes, on average, than those who don't.[2] Career or work is central to our well-being as adults emotionally as much as it is economically. And citizenship has to do with the responsibilities each of us must assume to keep the ship of society securely afloat.

I assert that conventional education can undermine performance in these three areas for two main reasons. First, schooling alienates youth from the educational process by focusing almost exclusively on academic subjects with little or no regard for their personal interests. Second, because schooling detaches learning from the context of real life, many youth fail to develop a clear purpose or mission for their lives. Instead, they pursue education as an end unto itself rather than as a means to a greater end. Both reasons can have serious consequences, as we shall see.

College

By the time they graduate from high school, many young people haven't the slightest clue about what to do with their lives. Some apply to college simply because it's what their parents expect of them. With no plan of their own, college becomes the default option for the next step in life. Then, once they've enrolled, they wander about, trying to decide on a major or field of study. Some end up spending at least a couple of years hopping from one field to another or even transferring institutions multiple times in search of a good match. Finding the "right" school does matter, as research suggests a correlation between student satisfaction and retention in higher education.[3] Eventually, some who wander do graduate but are just as lost as when they enrolled, in terms of career direction.

Unfortunately, all this shuffling around is costly in both time and money. Now, if you're an older advocate, you might readily recall the classic film *The Graduate*, which depicted the aimless life of a wealthy college graduate. Despite earning a degree from a prestigious university, he was nonetheless frustrated by a life without fulfillment or purpose. For the rest of my audience, allow me to share a relatively recent story that played out in my hometown, New Orleans.

After graduating from one of the city's top high schools, Robert Taylor was desperately trying to figure out his next move. Rather than following his initial instincts to pursue a career in criminal justice, he had chosen to study pharmacy as the result of encouraging conversations with a teacher during his senior year of high school. According to Robert, they talked about how the pharmacy program would lead to a good job and lifestyle, in material terms at least.

What eventually happened instead was frustratingly unfortunate. As it turned out, Robert hated the pharmacy program, performed poorly, and then dropped out after the first year. He decided to enroll at another college to pursue his passion in criminal justice and become a police officer. But as Murphy's law would have it, the first college would not release his transcript because he now owed $2,000, which was more than his low-income family could afford to pay. Without the transcript, the other college would not admit him. Talk about being caught between a rock and a hard place. Robert wistfully concluded, "I wish they would have pushed that more on us: What do you want to do?"[4] In other words, Robert felt he would have benefited from school a great deal more had his teachers and counselors helped him to figure out the "why?" of his education. Instead, school equipped him with technical knowledge and skills but with no purpose for applying them.

Unfortunately, his experience is far too common. While roughly 9 percent of youth enter college undecided on what field they intend to study, as many as 75 percent will change majors at least once during college.[5] The lack of direction that plagues many young people through high school can culminate into disengagement and debt when they attend college.

Ironically, even Robert's high school advisor echoed this crucial point, saying, "Too often students choose a major their parents like, that will give them a good career . . . only to flounder when they realize they don't like it . . . Then their grades suffer, and the students grow frustrated, bored or despondent."[6]

Are you beginning to grasp the magnitude of this problem of alienation from school? To put Robert's story into context, just listen to these astounding statistics highlighted by Ted Dintersmith in his illuminating work, *What School Could Be* (italics in the quoted material below are mine):

> Some 71% of 2015 college grads left with an average student loan debt of $35,000. A total of 43 million U.S. adults carry outstanding student loans that average $30,000, and some 25% are in default. Somewhat incredibly, 2.8 million adults aged sixty or older are still paying off their student loans . . . The financial overhang of college leads many young adults to steer clear of satisfying careers that offer modest salaries or doing anything as risky as starting their own business. *Conditioned* to jump through hoops and financially pressured, they trod to the career services office, apply for interviews, and take the highest-paying offer.[7]

Of course, not all persons with college loan debt also enrolled in the wrong school. Granted, some made a fine decision. Dintersmith's point, however, is that when saddled with so much debt, many young people no longer feel they can afford to pursue work that they enjoy but now must join the rat race instead.

Many students will tell you that both in high school and in college, they received far too little attention and guidance in career planning. Instead of incorporating career preparation at every step along the way, schools usually offer direct assistance only during a student's senior year as they prepare to graduate. Thus, many youth end up receiving a diploma for completing their studies without conceiving a plan for their future. Along my journey, however, I once heard that it is better to know where you are going and not know how than it is to know how but not know where you are going.

Sadly, many well-intentioned parents reinforce this lack of direction and purpose that many youth experience. Consider the remarks of one such parent as summarized by Carol Dweck in her landmark book *Mindset*:

> Let's look more closely at the message from Sandy's parents: *We don't care about who you are, what you're interested in, and what you can become. We don't care about learning. We will love and respect you only if you go to Harvard.*[8]

When parents think in this fashion, they end up advocating for the school instead of their child.

So, parents, educators, and other advocates, as a Harvard

alumnus, I'm going to let you in on a little secret. Are you listening? Good. I recall a survey that was done at my tenth reunion. When asked what had the greatest impact on our career success, most answered that our own efforts did—not the degree.

Moreover, at this point in my career, I would assert without a doubt that the further in time one's career advances, the less it matters where you went to school or what you majored in. In a sense then, the value of a degree itself diminishes over time. And although the value might never reach zero, in some instances, it might have a certain shelf life. Consider the following case in point.

Some years ago, a former classmate of mine decided to enroll in a master's degree program at a local college in New York City. He was utterly dismayed when he learned that the school would not grant credit for the courses he had completed for his bachelor's degree in economics from Harvard. Unless the degree had been earned within the last five years, they explained, he would have to take similar courses now to earn his master's degree. Begrudgingly, he anted up and took (or from his perspective, retook) the required courses.

More important than where or whether your child gets a degree, then, is the degree of their desire. Each year, roughly two million young people earn a college degree.[9] But without a connection to themselves to know what drives them, they drift. What matters most, therefore, is not the degree but the desire that inspires it. Thus, the shrewd youth advocate helps young people to pursue the former by developing the latter.

Career

Beyond working in the technology sector, what did Steve Jobs, Bill Gates, and Mark Zuckerberg all have in common? All three were college dropouts. They didn't stay in school to get their degrees; they left school to pursue their passions. And in doing so, went on to build companies that transformed the world and made billions of dollars in the process. The educational trajectories of these three titans of technology demonstrate that career takes priority over education—not the reverse. Consequently, if schooling helps to confuse rather than clarify a personal purpose or a career direction, then school is indeed getting in the way of the type of education that one needs to succeed.

Perhaps no story makes this point so clear as that of Steve Jobs himself, as revealed in his commencement speech of 2005 at Stanford University. Jobs explained why he dropped out of college: "After [the first] six months, I couldn't see the value in it. I had no idea what I wanted to do with my life and no idea how college was going to help me figure it out."[10] What he goes on to say is even more revealing. "It was one of the best decisions I ever made. The minute I dropped out I could stop taking the required classes that didn't interest me, and begin dropping in on the ones that looked interesting . . . I loved it. And much of what I stumbled into by following my curiosity and intuition turned out to be priceless later on." During that time, he gained insights that would prove valuable in his start-up business, Apple, ten years later.

Jobs's speech crescendos with several points that underscore the need for a new educational paradigm. He talks about how he overcame challenges early in his career, which included getting fired from the company he himself had created:

> Sometimes life hits you in the head with a brick. Don't lose faith. I'm convinced that the only thing that kept me going was that I loved what I did. You've got to find what you love. And that is as true for your work as it is for your lovers. Your work is going to fill a large part of your life, and the only way to be truly satisfied is to do what you believe is great work. And the only way to do great work is to love what you do . . . Don't let the noise of others' opinions drown out your own inner voice. And most important, have the courage to follow your heart and intuition. They somehow already know what you truly want to become. Everything else is secondary.[11]

Now, can you see the difference in the type of education Jobs pursued versus the conventional one that he rejected? His was inspired by passion, the other by tradition. And how did he excel professionally? By pursuing what he loved, which enabled his imagination and creativity to flow. Notably, Jobs saw his traditional college curriculum more as an impediment than a facilitator to developing his interests. From his eighteen-year-old perspective, which is the one that mattered, his college experience was too disconnected from the real world. Most importantly, it was also disconnected from Jobs. By its very design, college offered no clue as to how he might fulfill his passion, his potential, his purpose. In a word, college was academic.

Through the stories of both Steve Jobs and Robert Taylor, then, one may appreciate why this book is ultimately about the spiritual well-being of our youth. The conventional education they opposed sought to make them skillful but not willful. Its fundamental paradigm, "Cognition is king," nurtured them intellectually, yet it suppressed them emotionally. In both cases, education was aligned with standards but not with the students. Each of these stories epitomizes the harmful role that conventional education no doubt plays in the lives of thousands, if not millions, of young people every day, leading them away from rather than toward their greater selves.

Moreover, as implied at the beginning of this chapter, the alienation that youth experience in school cascades right on over into the workplace. Here, the consequences of alienation expand, costing U.S. companies lost productivity not only in trillions of dollars, but also in terms of employee morale. Consider this excerpt from a 2013 Gallup report:

> 70% of American workers are "not engaged" or "actively disengaged" and are emotionally disconnected from their workplaces and less likely to be productive . . . They are more likely to steal from their companies, negatively influence their coworkers, miss workdays, and drive customers away.[12]

And so, dear youth advocate, behind these stories we find what undoubtedly is the most nefarious consequence of conventional education. The greatest tragedy is not alienation from school but its potential offspring—*alienation from self*. Ever focused on gaining knowledge about academic subjects but not about themselves, many youth invariably lose their way, as did Robert Taylor. Worse yet, others never find their calling. Self-knowledge therefore is key. Fortunately, perhaps sensing this disconnect between education and success, Jobs was able to avoid alienation from self and pursued his passion relentlessly. I will return to the topic of self-knowledge later in the book.

Citizenship

Aside from empowering youth to fulfill their own lives, education should enable each of us to become better custodians of society. Preparing youth to become trustees of society should be an indispensable aim of the educational system, especially considering the growing social challenges confronting us. Diversity, climate change, the COVID-19 pandemic, and political polarization are a few examples, but let's get a deeper grasp of why citizenship matters.

Philosophies old and new have highlighted an important relationship between the role of education and the security of society. Though often attributed to Confucius, it was the Chinese statesman Guan Zhong who taught: "It takes ten years to grow a tree, but a hundred years to cultivate people."[13] Lincoln may have echoed a similar idea, as he allegedly proclaimed that the philosophy of the schoolroom in one generation becomes the philosophy of government in the next.[14] In short, the prosperity of a nation in the long run depends on the education of its citizenry.

Socrates was entirely skeptical about democracy as a system of government. Why? Because to function properly, democracy requires that the masses be able to think critically.[15] But without a means of providing such education for all, the ignorant in Greece had just as much of a say in political matters as did Socrates the philosopher. Thus, as long as the masses are ill-equipped to exercise critical thinking, the integrity of democracy remains in jeopardy. This is why John Dewey, one of America's most prominent philosophers of the twentieth century, referred to education as the midwife of democracy.[16]

In an effort to safeguard the new republic, Thomas Jefferson advocated strongly for public education. Jefferson felt that without a proper education, the common people might likely become prey to the manipulation of unscrupulous leaders.[17] A proper education, therefore, is one that encourages learners to think for themselves and to reason when formulating opinions as opposed to accepting an idea as true merely because someone else said so.

Also worthy of mention is that some notable philosophers have emphasized virtue as an essential element to a good life. This was certainly true of Plato, who also established the first institution of higher education in Greece.[18] And it was Rev. Dr. Martin L. King Jr. who once proclaimed: "Intelligence plus character—that is the true goal of education."[19] These great thinkers suggested that the development of virtue and character helps to promote the general welfare.

The need for such qualities also recognizes Kenyan philosopher John Mbiti's saying that "I am, because we are; and since we are therefore I am."[20] In other words, human existence is not isolated but interdependent. Therefore, without virtue, confidence in each other and in our social institutions naturally deteriorates.

Perhaps no other event has been as insightful regarding the need for critical thinking and virtue in education as the U.S. presidential election of 2020. I say so because this event brought to the forefront such momentous issues as the COVID-19 pandemic and climate change, not to mention the presidential election itself. The latter culminated with a violent attack on the U.S. Capitol on January 6, 2021. At least seven people died, 150 police were injured, and many more lives were threatened, including the vice president of the United States.[21] Now ask yourself plainly, should the facts of the aforementioned issues, or any others, vary among educators as they do among politicians?

Topics like the aforementioned offer prime opportunities for transforming social studies in particular, and education in general, from seemingly irrelevant to absolutely meaningful. And no matter the educator's political perspective, he or she should guide students in distinguishing facts from opinions on any topic. Doing so might be accomplished by starting with clear and practical questions. For example: "What evidence does the scientific community rely on to assess climate change?

How might we as ordinary citizens determine if the pandemic is real, or whether our presidential election results are valid?" After students have properly researched a topic, then allow them to formulate their own opinions. And, of course, an assessment would never be based on their opinion itself, but on how well they supported it. Regardless of political affiliation, I contend that it is the responsibility of the youth advocate to teach students *how to think*—not *what to think*.

Unfortunately, in many communities, the educational system sits on the sideline muted when it is most needed. This inattention to issues so vital to society's welfare is clear evidence of schooling's academic nature, its detachment from real life, and consequently its perceived irrelevance to youth.

School's detachment from social concerns promotes apathy and irresponsibility. As evidence, one out of every three Americans did not vote in the 2020 U.S. presidential election. And some schools will suspend students who become civically active.[22] It is unsurprising, therefore, that citizens eighteen to twenty-four years of age had the lowest level of votership (51 percent) in the 2020 election.[23] Thus, conventional education shuts the school door to the real world while it encourages students to focus on acquiring the academic skills to pass college entrance examinations. Moreover, they are conditioned to secure good jobs in the short term, while neglecting the basic responsibilities of citizenship needed to secure the society that sustains their jobs in the long run.

Educators who recognize, as philosophers have, the connection between education and society will say, "Bring it on!"

rather than distort or ignore reality. Aristotle, for example, allegedly said: "It is the mark of an educated mind to be able to entertain a thought without accepting it."[24] Therefore, bring in the diverse perspectives! For by limiting them, do we not also limit our education? And what about the book banning in education today? Well, as has been said, he who controls the diameter of one's education controls the circumference of their thinking. Moreover, is it not within the educator's purview to dispel the darkness of ignorance and fear through the light of knowledge and reason? Then why not bring in the scholars as well so that students can learn to debate ideas, detect falsehood, and discern truth? Otherwise, of this we can be certain: In human affairs, fear often trumps reason. But whenever one's perspective is driven by the former rather than the latter, then one's corresponding actions are likely to limit personal development and achievement. For just as our muscles grow when pushed beyond their comfort zone, our potential for success increases when we practice new and creative ways of thinking.

Unfortunately, history suggests that teaching about controversial issues will always be challenging, to say the least. Remember what Socrates, the father of Western philosophy himself, was accused of and sentenced to death for in Athens more than two thousand years ago? "Corrupting the youth."[25] (As the saying goes . . . Some things never change.) Yet, only when our young people develop the ability to evaluate controversial issues for themselves will they be prepared to uphold democracy. On that point, I'm sure Socrates, Jefferson, and Dewey would agree.

AUTHOR'S KEY POINTS

1. The consequences of alienation in school are costly and far-reaching.
2. Alienation from school can diminish one's performance not only in education, but also in career and civic responsibility.
3. Ultimately, alienation from school may result in something far worse: alienation from self. This state may impair one's ability to find meaning and purpose throughout one's entire life.

MY KEY REFLECTIONS

1. What in this chapter left the biggest impression on me?

2. What personal experiences, if any, did this chapter bring to mind?

3. What action might I or others take based on what I've learned?

CHAPTER 4

Reality Check: Insights from School Leaders

Remember that education is a matter of the heart.

—**St. John Bosco, Italian educator and priest**

In the previous chapters, I have spent time explaining the problem of alienation from school. However, you might also be asking yourself, "But what's the alternative to conventional schooling or the so-called Broccoli Model? Pie in the sky, right?" Wrong. Recognizing that some opponents of the paradigm shift for which I advocate will discredit it as wishful thinking, in this chapter and the rest of this book, I'll be pushing the envelope. I'm going to make this ideal real. My wish for you, the youth advocate, is to understand fully that the idea of transforming education is far more practical than one might think. In this chapter, therefore, I'm going to share what I learned from several educators right here in my own backyard.

I should disclose that at the point of interviewing these educators prior to the COVID-19 pandemic, I intended for this book to serve as a guide solely for parents. That changed, however, as my research continued. Eventually, I switched the book's focus to youth advocates in general, which includes parents. Nonetheless, I wanted to hear from educators themselves about this unsettling scenario, familiar to most of us as simply the way education is. I wanted to know how important, if at all, did school leaders think it was to provide more than just academic rigor. So, in this chapter, I'm going to share what a handful of local school leaders had to say regarding that topic. I'm delighted to say up front that I was quite pleased and even a bit surprised by what I found.

As for my approach, I contacted heads of schools in the metropolitan New Orleans area directly by telephone and email. I relied on a list of private schools, believing they would be relatively easy to access. In addition, I reached out to several superintendents of public school districts. Eight administrators accepted my invitation for an interview. All but one of these were at private schools. Despite the diversity of their educational programs, all had reputations locally for educational excellence.

Three of my major interview questions addressed student achievement, engagement, and emotional development:

1. How do you get the excellent results that your school has produced over the years?
2. What challenges do you experience in achieving those outcomes?
3. How important are student engagement and emotional development to school administrators?

Innocuous enough, don't you agree? But then fairly early into the interview, I politely began to ask more pointed questions. I also highlighted some of the stats on student engagement cited earlier in this book. Importantly, I also asked: "What, in your opinion, is the school administration's role or responsibility in addressing student engagement and the emotional development of students?" And, not holding back on any punches, I piggybacked on Sir Robinson's TED Talk (chapter 1) by asking: "How would you respond to the notion that school kills creativity?"

Following is a summary of the key findings and takeaways that I consider most pertinent to this book. School leaders attributed their excellence in education to providing an educational program—comprised of both academic and nonacademic instruction. Moreover, they accomplish their excellence primarily through effective teachers. As for challenges, two major obstacles surfaced among the administrators: (1) finding good teachers and (2) changes in society.

When it comes to good teachers, all the administrators suggested that knowledge of subject matter alone is insufficient.

Don't Let School Get in the Way of Education

They expressed a need to find individuals who also are caring and concerned about helping youth to become good people. And, as you might imagine, each school had its idea of what a "good" person was as well as its own formula for cultivating one. All school leaders put a pretty good degree of emphasis on teacher training, and they seemed fairly diverse in their approaches.

As for societal changes, our conversations enlivened at times, as some administrators talked about how attitudes among parents and students have changed over time. As an example, one shared a cartoon, which I found absolutely hilarious. It portrayed parents in 1960 blaming their child for getting poor grades in school versus in 2010, parents—along with their child—blaming the teacher![1]

Actually, I could relate to that one personally from my own experience as a teacher. My first regular teaching job was fifth grade in the New Orleans Public Schools. I had just earned my master's in education from Teachers College, Columbia University, in New York City. At "Parents' Night" near the beginning of the school year, I was enthusiastically presenting my instructional plan, explaining how I hoped to take their children to the next level academically. During the question period afterward, one parent with hand on hip abruptly exclaimed: "We appreciate all you've been learning up on the East Coast, but as a teacher myself, I'm concerned that my child isn't getting any homework." Luckily for me, before I could respond, another parent interjected: "Really? That's interesting. I was going to express concern that maybe my child was getting too much homework." Thus, without my uttering a single word, it became apparent to everyone in the room that the child of the first parent had been telling her mother that I was not assigning homework. That parent, who had believed her daughter without question, remained silent the rest of the meeting.

So, although I'm a staunch advocate for youth empowerment, I'm just as adamant about youth assuming personal responsibility. And, for their own sake, I urge you to do the same.

Now, let's get to key question number 3: How important are student engagement and emotional development to school administrators? And in what ways, if any, do they develop students emotionally or nonacademically?

In sum, I am delighted to say that the insights shared by school leaders in my interviews were absolutely amazing! Although they varied significantly in their approaches, all of them expressed a great deal of concern about engaging students at school as well as concern for their social and emotional development. I might even describe their opinions about developing youth academically without attention to their attitudes as tantamount to making a cake without baking powder: They simply won't rise to their potential.

Mind you, however, that my sample of school administrators was small and not representative of all schools in the United States. Seven out of the eight schools were private, and six of those had a religious affiliation (mostly Catholic). Nationally, however, 9 percent of students attend private schools.[2] Another limitation was that the information I gathered reflected the *opinions* of the school leaders. Those opinions were not necessarily the *practices* of educators within those schools. To compensate for this limitation, I did ask the administrators how they assessed their nonacademic outcomes. Again, I was pleased to hear their responses. With that said, now I'm going to highlight some of the ideas and insights that I found so inspiring.

Take a look at the mission statement of Metairie Park Country Day School, where my first meeting took place:

> Our students learn to be flexible, to be adaptable, and to face the challenges of life with honor, optimism, confidence, creativity, and a sense of humor.[3]

The last part of that sentence caught me totally by surprise: "a sense of humor." I mean, how often do you see that in a school? After an inviting conversation, the head of school took me on an absolutely beautiful tour of the campus. While we stood observing the instruction in one classroom in the upper school, I was surprised again when a student popped up out of his seat, walked over to us, introduced himself, and began explaining the lesson to me. *Wow!* I thought. *Now, that's what I call a school mission in action.* But was it really? Or perhaps I had just missed the head of school, who was several inches taller than me, signaling the boy to come over? Based on my overall impression of the school's climate, I remain willing to conclude that it was the former.

During my next interview, which took place at Jesuit High

School for boys, I found more concern than expected for the emotional development of students. In response to the research I presented about boredom in classrooms, the administrator declared that they worked at reducing traditional instruction as part of an eight-year initiative that studied skillful teaching.[4] Amazing! Moreover, to cultivate character development, he explained that their requirement for community service was not focused on hours but on outcomes (e.g., religious values and caring for others). To my delight, I even learned that they assess these outcomes through student surveys and essays. "In this way," he explained, "we educate 'men of faith and men for others'" (the school's mission).[5]

My next trip took me to St. Augustine High School, highly regarded especially within the city's African American community. I was fortunate enough to catch the school's president and principal. Here's the gist of what they had to say on this topic: "The cognitive, affective, and spiritual domains are most important to us . . . We have rigor, but it appears students experience fulfillment from extracurriculars [e.g., band, sports, clubs]. *And as a bonus, it motivates them to perform academically.* [my italics]."[6] Their remarks clearly underscore the connection between emotion and achievement rather than intellect alone. The value they placed on developing young men spiritually, emotionally, as well as academically came across as nothing less than paramount.

I found similar ideas regarding education at Northlake Christian School. Moreover, both the head of school and principal indicated that they provided professional development to change traditional views on how to teach. Unfortunately, but unsurprisingly, they also described one of their biggest challenges in developing students as "a teacher mindset resistant to change."[7] In emphasizing this point, they made me aware of an excellent resource that any educator or advocate can use to bring excitement to learning, a book entitled *Teach Like a PIRATE* by Dave Burgess. Having worked in many education reform initiatives myself, I couldn't agree more with the importance these two school leaders placed on not only finding but also developing good teachers.

The headmaster at John Curtis Christian School put a great deal of emphasis on developing a sense of community. With fewer than one hundred students per grade (kindergarten to grade twelve), he explained:

> We don't want to be so large that we don't know our kids. It's a family environment . . . I want them to feel involved. Intrinsic involvement outside of the classroom is key, in my opinion. Schools need to provide open environments that encourage this. I think the whole educational process should help you to find yourself.[8]

The latter, as we shall see, is also an idea that I embrace wholeheartedly. I was also fascinated that he concurrently filled the role of football coach (and previously basketball and baseball). "Athletics . . . I believe is an extension of the classroom and the process of teaching," he explained. Accordingly, the lobby to his office was decorated with a sparkling display of trophies from championships in sports at both local and state levels.

One of the most enlightening conversations of all came through my interview with the headmaster of Archbishop Shaw High School. Still, at this very moment, I can easily recall his peaceful and calm demeanor. He made me feel so at ease, I could have listened to him talk for the rest of the day. I was particularly intrigued by the school's nonacademic values, which he referred to as the "Preventive System of Education: Reason, Religion, Kindness, and Active Presence."[9] After learning about the historical and philosophical origins of this system, I developed a deep appreciation for the school's emphasis on educating "the whole person" spiritually, socially, emotionally, as well as intellectually.[10] So even though the school's mission focused on academic achievement, I left the interview with a sense that students were expected to graduate with much more than just college and career preparation. How befitting, then, is this quote by St. John Bosco, founder of the school's philosophy: "Remember that education is a matter of the heart."[11]

Coincidentally, this idea reappeared in another interview, this time with the head administrator at Cabrini High School for girls.[12] Reflecting the school's mission to educate the minds and hearts of young women, their slogan for educational outcomes became one of my favorites: "Find friendship, find faith, find your future."[13] What a beautiful concept! Our conversation was most enjoyable. In fact, it was in his office that I found the cartoon mentioned at the beginning of this chapter.

Last, I had the honor of meeting with the superintendent of Plaquemines Parish School Board, one of the smallest yet highest-achieving districts in the area. The superintendent's insights were particularly appreciated given his revelation that he himself was a "C student" in school. Aside from finding good teachers, one of the greatest challenges he expressed was "getting kids to see themselves as capable of anything."[14] This is yet another theme stressed in this book. The superintendent also shared that his desire to meet the needs of all students was heavily influenced by personal experiences as the area went through the civil rights era decades earlier. As I understood him, the inequity that permeated education as well as society at that time fueled his personal sense of fairness with a desire and commitment to ensure a quality education for all. Thus, I contend both his experience and approach underscore the notion that passion propels performance.

So, there you have it. What do I conclude about the dire picture of education portrayed by some researchers and students, based on my conversations with a small group of local school leaders? To begin, like anything else, schools are diverse. As a result of my interviews, I definitely believe that many educators not only recognize the importance of their students' emotional well-being but also encourage it.

Although the Broccoli Model rules in American education, clearly there are exceptions. Moreover, the aforementioned examples suggest that a new paradigm that calls for making schools more responsive to the emotional needs of youth is not "pie in the sky" but already present in the here and now. The problem is that there aren't enough of them. So, if you happen to be a parent shopping for a school in the New Orleans area, those that I visited might be some good options to consider.

That being said, in the next chapter, I provide an overview of my personally developed framework for creating great schools. It's based on what I refer to as "PMM: the Pumpkin Muffin Model."

AUTHOR'S KEY POINTS

1. Despite the national landscape covered by student disengagement, there are schools that address the emotional development of youth in excellent ways.

2. Smaller enrollments coupled with greater independence from state regulations may offer some private schools an advantage over other schools, in terms of addressing the emotional needs of students.

3. Regardless of school type or sector, leadership is a key ingredient that determines how well an institution addresses the emotional needs of youth.

MY KEY REFLECTIONS

1. What in this chapter left the biggest impression on me?

2. What personal experiences, if any, did this chapter bring to mind?

3. What action might I or others take based on what I've learned?

CHAPTER 5

A New Paradigm for Education

The mind is not a vessel to be filled but a fire to be kindled.
—**Plutarch, Greek philosopher and historian**

Thus far, we have found the national education landscape pervaded by youth alienated from schooling. This problem, maintained by what I call the Broccoli Model of Education, threatens the success of youth from all backgrounds. We explored an insightful and deeply painful story about the schooling of one adolescent to demonstrate how serious the consequences of conventional education can be. Then, we learned some of the typical ways conventional schooling may undermine the well-being of millions of students, workers, and society as a whole. In the previous chapter, however, we observed how some schools do address the nonacademic needs of youth right here and now. The chapter at hand takes us yet a step further, laying the foundation for a new paradigm in education.

The foundation of this new paradigm is formed out of the challenges we've discussed thus far, but even more so, it's based on what an ideal education could be. Let us begin by clarifying our expectations of an ideal education by asking some key questions. They involve topics we hardly discuss, ones we often take for granted but which are extremely important. Why? Because the answers to the following questions are what drive our expectations and actions. (1) What is education? (2) What is its purpose? and (3) What should the educational process look like to achieve that purpose?

Now, for those who are afraid that I might waste time with philosophical talk, allow me to suggest why these questions matter.

I can remember sitting in one of those grandiose lecture halls on campus one day during my first year as a student at Harvard. While gazing distractedly at the beauty of the hall's ornate walls, not to mention that of a female classmate or two seated in the distance, I could hear my sociology professor discussing the philosophy of Karl Marx. At one point, she asked rather deliberately: "What is work?" The question immediately arrested my nineteen-year-old brain, and I began to rebel. *What kind of ridiculous question is that?* I thought. *Everybody knows that work is simply something you gotta do. Gee whiz! These folks are gettin' just a little bit too intellectual for me. Maybe I ought to be thinking about changing my major.*

Now, can you see how that attitude, how that perspective

might have affected my performance? Can you see how my concept of work itself might have influenced how I approached my studies—or worse yet, my career? Clearly, what I needed was not a change of major but a change of mind. I hope, therefore, that you appreciate why I now must ask you the first of the big three questions . . .

What Is Education?

The definition that most of us are probably familiar with sounds something like this: "to provide schooling for" or "to train by formal instruction and supervised practice especially in a skill, trade, or profession."[1] These are the first two definitions found in *Merriam-Webster*'s online dictionary. Both definitions imply a couple of things about the relationship between teaching and learning. One, the student must receive or acquire knowledge. Two, the student thus becomes the object of instruction. *Merriam-Webster* adds that "educate implies development of the mind."[2]

Now, juxtapose all that to the opening quote at the beginning of this chapter made by Plutarch of ancient Greece. In one of his works, *Moralia*, he elaborates on this idea: "For the mind does not require filling like a bottle, but rather, like wood, it only requires kindling to create in it an impulse to think independently and an ardent desire for the truth." Plutarch's insight thus seems particularly applicable to our times, given that we have seen how schooling often extinguishes rather than ignites the fire of imagination and creativity in youth.

Don't Let School Get in the Way of Education

Right here is where we begin to see the truth of my assertion made in the book's introduction, that education is ultimately a spiritual matter. When guided by the conventional definitions of education, students become the passive recipients of instruction that we witness today. Plutarch's kindling of a fire, however, is consistent with the word *educe* (to bring out something latent), which stems from the Latin origin of educate: *educere*, meaning to lead forth.[3] In other words, by kindling the mind rather than merely filling it, the educational process inspires independent thinking and a desire to learn more, and thus become more.

Such inspiration and desire may be summarized in one word—enthusiasm. *Merriam-Webster* defines enthusiasm as: "a strong excitement of feeling, something inspiring zeal or fervor." Now, doesn't that sound like the kindling of a fire? The meaning of enthusiasm and its essential role in education become even more clear when we consider the word's etymology. In his enlightening book *Aspire*, Kevin Hall quotes his mentor, Professor Arthur R. Watkins, as explaining: "Originating with the Greeks, 'enthusiasm' means *God within* or *God's gifts within*. . . . It refers to the divine light that shines within each of us."[4] Now, I ask you, what could be more spiritual than that?

Who would deny that the divine light of enthusiasm—fully visible in children during kindergarten—gets snuffed out of many by the time they reach high school? Conventional schooling slowly and subtly extinguishes enthusiasm—the God within—the fervor and creative potential that resides in each of us. Conventional schooling was the force that alienated the genius of Steve Jobs, that overwhelmingly frustrated the desire to learn in Jeff Bliss, and that gnawed away the zeal of young Edmund Perry. The same is true for millions of young people, as evidenced through student surveys. And if you disregard this warning, your child may be the next to join them: Never let school get in the way of education!

I believe it is imperative, therefore, that students' emotions be given the utmost attention in education. Filling the mind like a bottle alludes to conventional schooling where teachers aim merely to impart academic knowledge and skills. In contrast, kindling a fire is when teachers relate knowledge and skills to students in a way that not only informs but also inspires them. Thus, whereas conventional schooling emphasizes what educators call "the delivery of instruction," Plutarch's idea underscores the need for teachers to develop the learner's perspective. How we see ourselves and the world directly influences our thoughts, feelings, and actions, which in turn will make or break our lives. Or as Zig Ziglar said: "Your attitude, not your aptitude, will determine your altitude."[5]

In my humble opinion then, education may be defined simply as the cultivation of one's mind through the development of knowledge, skills, and enthusiasm.

What Is the Purpose of Education?

So, to what end does one cultivate the mind? For what purpose do we acquire and develop knowledge, skills, and perspective? Why should youth spend years—and their parents, thousands of dollars—on education?

Don't Let School Get in the Way of Education

In a word, the purpose of education is empowerment. To empower is to enhance one's ability to be effective, to exercise greater control and influence over one's life. The beauty of this purpose is that it does not dictate specifically how one should live other than to suggest that education should help one to live well. And most of us would likely agree that living well is multifaceted. Education therefore should enhance one's ability to improve one's quality of life. In practical terms, that means enjoying good physical and mental health, fulfilling work, supportive relationships, financial security, exercising personal as well as social responsibility, and so forth. In short, the purpose of education is not to get a good job but to lead a better life.

In light of its benefits, youth advocates should be mindful of efforts at home and abroad to restrict access to education. Historically, the education of girls, for example, has often been curtailed if not neglected entirely. Their access to education has been diminished, I would argue, for the same reason that here in the United States it was once illegal to teach enslaved Africans to read. Generally speaking, to educate is to empower. (Recall, however, that I had a lot to say in chapter 3 about what it means to be properly educated.)

I will talk more about empowerment in the book's final chapter. But for now, this brings us to our third and final big question.

What Should the Educational Process Look Like?

To address this question, I believe we must once again entertain some philosophical ideas. But don't worry. I will do so, as always, with a practical touch.

Thus far, I have described the conventional approach to education as the Broccoli Model. This metaphor has proven powerful in my professional development workshops for educators. To their dismay, I walk down the aisle with a bowl of raw broccoli doused in soymilk. This striking image embodies the erroneous belief that in order to be rigorous, education must be unpalatable.

Now, to describe the educational process under a new paradigm, I'm going to give you an apt and delectable alternative to the Broccoli Model—something specific and concrete. Something you not only can wrap your hands around but also sink your teeth into. Drum roll, please . . . Ladies and gentlemen, I hereby present to you the Pumpkin Muffin Model!

The Pumpkin Muffin Model embodies the idea that schooling can be rigorous—and at the same time, enjoyable. The metaphor thus symbolizes the paradigm shift that I believe is necessary to take education to another level, the kind needed for the twenty-first-century child. To demonstrate what the educational process should look like under this new paradigm, let's contrast it with the current paradigm. The subsequent table highlights the differences between the Broccoli and Pumpkin approaches to education.

When contrasting the two perspectives, please keep in mind

this important point: I propose the Pumpkin Muffin Model as an alternative and creative approach for optimal youth development. In other words, I don't deny that a regular diet with broccoli and soy milk—if you can stomach it—is likely to have positive health benefits. Similarly, the academic rigor typically served in schools can improve your child's knowledge and skills. But if schools were to emphasize both nutritional value *and* taste, in other words rigor *and* emotional fulfillment, that would be a game changer. It would lead to a far more effective educational process, one that would inspire rather than alienate many more students.

Now, let's contrast the two approaches to education in order to bring some clarity to our third big question (see Figure 5).

Entire books have been written about the nature of our educational system, but here's my hundred-word summary: Driven mainly by needs of the economy, conventional schooling primarily seeks to equip youth with technical knowledge and skills. Accordingly, school focuses on cognitive development through academic subjects, and innate ability is revered as the source of achievement. Thus, the coveted designation of "gifted and talented" is conferred only upon a chosen few. For efficiency, instruction is delivered in a machine-like fashion, and assessments are used to categorize students. To enhance efficiency, school demands compliance and conformity; consequently, a child's natural motivation to learn becomes extrinsic. In turn, students experience alienation from school. Increasingly, they disengage, and underachievement naturally follows.

A New Paradigm for Education

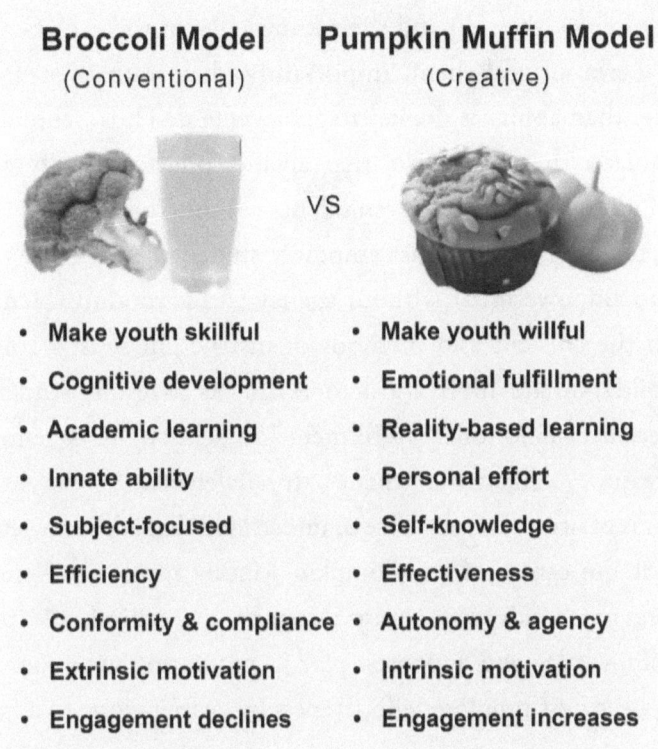

Figure 5. Contrasts between Conventional and Creative Schooling. By author; images from the training video that I produced personally for YouTube. (See https://youtu.be/-JCgcV2iqJQ.)⁶

Now, let's consider the alternative to the Broccoli Model, the Pumpkin Muffin approach: Based on principles of human effectiveness, the creative approach to schooling primarily seeks to empower students by aiding them in finding a sense of purpose, equipped with the knowledge and skills to realize it. Accordingly, school focuses on the emotional fulfillment of students through reality-based activities. And by doing so, they expand their knowledge of themselves and the world around them. Importantly, they learn that effort rather than ability is the key to achievement. Thus, schooling stimulates the enthusiasm that enables one to identify and then cultivate the God-given talents within. To be considered effective, the school must empower students. And there can be no empowerment without agency and autonomy. Hence, both the content and methods of instruction must harness a child's innate motivation to learn. As a result, students experience emotional fulfillment at school. Engagement increases . . . and achievement naturally ensues.

It is of utmost importance to understand that self-knowledge lies at the center of the Pumpkin Muffin approach. Here is where youth advocates must recognize the critical role that self-knowledge and awareness play in promoting one's success. Self-awareness promotes effectiveness by enabling one to adjust their activities based on one's personal strengths and weaknesses. Media mogul Oprah Winfrey beautifully illustrates this idea through her personal story as both a child and an adult. For example, as a kindergarten student she had the self-awareness to recognize her advanced vocabulary.[7] She explained to her teacher that she felt out of place, and consequently, the principal promoted her to first grade. In her career as well, Oprah attributes much of her success to self-awareness.

The advocate also must recognize that a pivotal aspect of self-knowledge is one's perspective. Stephen Covey, one of the most perspicacious thinkers of our time, contended, "We must look *at* the lens through which we see the world, as well as

A New Paradigm for Education

at the world we see, and that the lens itself shapes how we interpret the world."[8] Thus, by becoming aware of our own paradigms, we can become more effective in life; for our paradigms, he explained, are the source of our attitudes and behaviors. Consider, for instance, my own paradigm about work, described at the beginning of this chapter.

Developing awareness about one's own paradigms also has very practical implications when it comes to issues pertaining to diversity, equity, and inclusion (DEI), which I mentioned at the beginning of chapter 2. In my humble opinion, no one expresses this idea as well as Covey:

> It is extremely valuable to train the mind to stand apart and examine its own program . . . Training, without such education, narrows and closes the mind so that the assumptions underlying the training are never examined. That's why it is so valuable to read broadly and to expose yourself to great minds.[9]

What, for example, might Covey's insight suggest about the policy of book banning, mentioned in chapter 3? Further, does not his contention also imply that current efforts nationwide to exclude diverse perspectives from curriculum and instruction will only cripple students' ability to examine their own assumptions and thinking? And if such efforts demand conformity and compliance in perspective, then do they not foster bias and thus blindness (see chapter 2), rather than the light needed to see that one's own perspective is not necessarily the truth, but instead one of many possible versions of it? Therefore, if school limits rather than expands the perspectives of youth—precisely at a time when social diversity is increasing—then it seems certain that school is getting in the way of the education youth need to succeed. For bias and blindness lead not to understanding and cooperation but to ignorance, conflict, and chaos.

Finally, the reader should note that the contrasts between the Broccoli and Pumpkin Muffin approaches to education stem from two different theoretical perspectives. Consistent with the current system's emphasis on cognitive development, curriculum and instruction in many, if not most, schools today operate largely from the ideas of Jean Piaget, one of the most influential psychologists of the twentieth century. Piaget's theory of cognitive development does indeed provide an efficient and useful framework for delivering instruction. According to his theory, from birth to about age twelve the mind goes through four predictable stages of development. By understanding the mind's capabilities at each stage, educators can reliably organize instruction in ways that students are likely to comprehend.

The creative educational approach described heretofore operates from a theoretical perspective quite different from Piaget's. Whereas the current educational paradigm emphasizes the role of cognitive development in learning, the self-determination theory (SDT), which we discussed in chapter 2, stresses the role of social interaction. Allow me to reintroduce and expand on the theory here to make a clearer contrast between the two approaches to education. SDT asserts that human beings have an innate desire to learn in order to direct their own lives. The fulfillment of that desire is influenced by our psychological needs for relatedness, competence, and autonomy. Relatedness has to do with the feeling of belonging or attachment to others. Competence is about one's feeling of effectiveness, and autonomy refers to one's need for a sense of control or self-expression. Importantly, environments that help one to meet these needs promote one's engagement, which facilitates learning; similarly, environments that thwart these needs discourage engagement and thus stymie learning. From an SDT perspective, then, the social context of school, rather than cognitive capacity, is key in determining student achievement.

As will become evident in the chapters forthcoming, self-determination theory aptly forms a foundation for the new paradigm that I propose in this book. It explains how the social environment impacts human behavior. Moreover, SDT underscores empowerment as the overarching purpose of education.

Two Steps Toward a New Paradigm for Education

George Bernard Shaw famously said, "You see things; and you say, 'Why?' But I dream things that never were; and I say, 'Why not?'"[10] Accordingly, here is the first of two challenges I put before you that could usher in the paradigm shift from the Broccoli Model of Education to the Pumpkin Muffin Model. Now that we have answered the three big questions in education, I challenge you to imagine schooling as a process that becomes increasingly engaging.

What would it look like if your child were to leave high school even more energetic and enthusiastic than when they entered kindergarten? What if your daughter didn't lose any of her curiosity and creativity? What if your son were to retain that sense of possibility and excitement, and then couple them with technical knowledge, skills, and an "I CAN!" attitude? Your kids would be ready and able to conquer the world, wouldn't they? And just think about how prospective colleges and future employers might react to young people with such acute minds and indomitable spirits!

So, in contrast to the current national picture where student engagement declines through schooling, I first challenge you to envision an educational system where engagement increases over time. Why not? Consider this contrast (see Figure 6), based on what I presented in chapter 1.

My second challenge to you as a parent or youth advocate has the potential to be even more seismic. For many of you, this may mean feeling some discomfort by placing yourself in opposition to the prevailing educational system. I'm sorry. But for the betterment of our youth, I challenge you to embrace the idea that your child is *gifted*! Nationwide, the Broccoli Model of Education confers this designation on only about 6 percent of all students.[11] Moreover, it does so by using a variety of different formulas, depending on the state or the local community.[12] Ironically, therefore, if your child crossed the border between or even within states, they might lose their status. What does that suggest to you about the validity of that designation?

A New Paradigm for Education

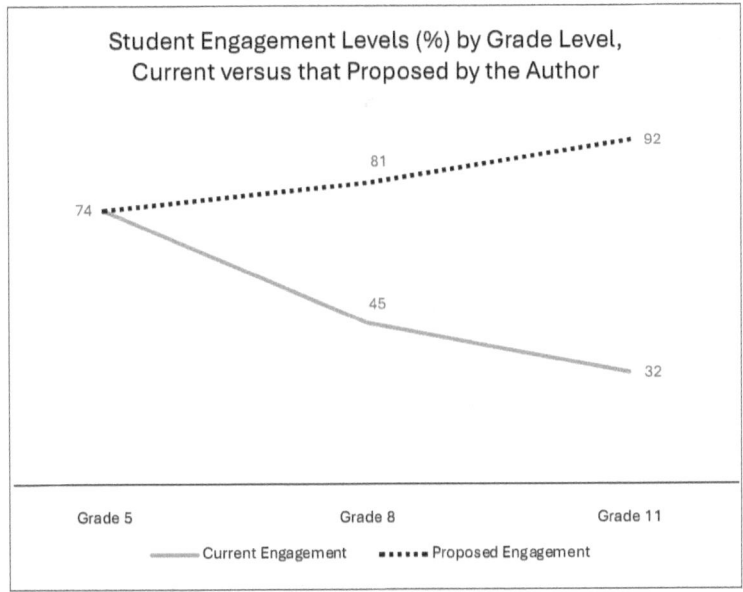

Figure 6. Source of Current Levels of Student Engagement: 2016 Gallup Student Poll.[13]

The effect of embracing this idea could be as powerful for you now as it was originally for researchers and educators in 1964. At that time, a Harvard psychologist named Robert Rosenthal conducted a teacher experiment whose outcome became known as the Pygmalion effect.[14] At the beginning of the school year, Rosenthal labeled some of the students as "bloomers" (above average in intelligence), when in fact it was not true, based on their IQ score. By the end of the year, however, those students outperformed their peers when they all took the same IQ test again. Rosenthal explained that the teachers' belief in the labels changed their expectations and actions, which in turn improved their students' performance.

Now I challenge you to do the same. Embrace the idea

that the youth whom you serve, or your own children for that matter, are indeed gifted, though not necessarily as defined by any school. Instead, I am advocating that you believe them to be gifted and talented, as many "successful" people would undoubtedly agree that they are. In contrast to educators who typically rely on standardized test scores to identify talent, high achievers outside of education place greater emphasis on passion, hard work, and persistence as predictors of achievement. Many of them would also tell you that all of us can be great at something. That something is your gift. The challenge for each of us is to discover our gifts and then align them with meaningful and fulfilling work. But if you cling to a label that does not empower you to begin with, then your gifts may never flourish.

You need not depend on the educational system to confer this honor upon your youth. Confer it upon them yourself. And then, treat them accordingly. Nurturing them in that way over time will almost guarantee their success.

But now it's time to make a decision. Make it a personal declaration today right here and now. If you work with youth, then make this a formal declaration in your educational program. Of course, share it with all staff members as well as parents. Insist that they respect the declaration and interact with your young people accordingly. If you are just a parent, however, then grab a pen and fill in the following page for each of your children. And in time, they will rise to the level of expectation.

Having sufficiently discussed the why and how of establishing a new paradigm for education, let's move on. The rest of this book will provide five ways of making schooling an engaging rather than alienating experience. Combined, I refer to them as the five features of the FACES framework (Fun, Affirmation, Challenge, Expression, and Success). And, as we shall see, the next chapter, Fun, sets the stage for igniting the God-given passion within each of us.

My Child Has a Gift

"On this day, _____, as a parent who
(date)
believes deeply in the power of positive expectations, I hereby declare that my child,

_____,
(name)
is gifted with something special to give to the world.

And although I may not yet know what that special gift is, I pledge and dedicate myself to helping my child to discover and develop her/his passions, talents, and interests, so that he/she may have the best chance for a happy and fulfilling life!"

Parent/Guardian: _____
(signature)

You may download a free copy of this declaration at: DrOinspires.com.

AUTHOR'S KEY POINTS

1. This book proposes a new paradigm for education based on passion and emotional fulfillment, rather than cognitive ability and development.

2. In contrast to the Broccoli Model of chapter 1, the Pumpkin Muffin Model is a metaphor for making schooling enjoyable as well as rigorous.

3. The new paradigm summarized as "passion propels performance!" means that success in life has more to do with emotional fulfillment than with intellectual ability.

4. FACES is a framework for implementing the proposed new education paradigm. Incorporating its five features—Fun, Affirmation, Challenge, Expression, and Success—into educational programs will help to ensure that all youth thrive.

MY KEY REFLECTIONS

1. What in this chapter left the biggest impression on me?

2. What personal experiences, if any, did this chapter bring to mind?

3. What action might I or others take based on what I've learned?

Part II

CHAPTER 6

Fun: Enjoyment of Learning

To make real progress in preparing all students to succeed in the twenty-first century, schools need to tap into the passions of students.

—**Wagner and Dintersmith, authors,** *Most Likely to Succeed*

The first feature of the FACES framework is "Fun." As far as our topic is concerned, fun means that the learning process overall should be enjoyable. Now, note my choice of words here carefully. I have said "the learning process overall." I believe students should experience, in general, a sense of emotional fulfillment and joy in schooling, rather than the alienation and boredom that so many complain about.

One should not misconstrue my words, however, to suggest

that every day, all day long, students should pass their time laughing endlessly and engaging mindlessly in play. Instead, I simply mean that students should find pleasure in their activities at school more often than not. For any time that we, as human beings, get to experience activities that inspire pleasure, the incentive to engage naturally follows. And with persistence, engagement leads to achievement.

Although I believe education has come a long way regarding the idea of kids having fun at school, this is still where many educators are ready to get off the bus. Based on what we know students typically say about their classrooms, the phrase "joyful education" seems to be but an oxymoron. In fact, one of the most hilarious examples of this perspective of education was depicted in the movie *Matilda* (1996), based on the book of that title by the acclaimed author Roald Dahl.[1] It portrayed a stocky elementary school principal wearing military-like attire with a whip in hand, standing ominously before the classroom with this inscription over the blackboard:

> "IF YOU ARE HAVING FUN,
> YOU ARE NOT LEARNING."

While not nearly as dramatic as the movie, here's an anecdote from real life that underscores the same point.

An article from the *Washington Post* in 2009 titled "Schools Need Teachers Like Me. I Just Can't Stay" tells the story of Sarah Fine's brief tenure as a high school English teacher in the District of Columbia.[2] The school's culture was pervaded by the kind of apathy among students that has been discussed throughout this book. Still, on account of her passion and commitment to making a difference, Ms. Fine persisted. On one particular day, however, her frustration reached a new level. Her tenth-grade class was abuzz with excitement. Then, one of the school administrators passed by, assessed the situation, and commanded Fine to get her class "seated and silent." The message was clear: With all that noise and moving about in the classroom, how could students possibly be learning anything?!

Now ask yourself, do we not in general, as human beings, participate more deeply, engage longer, work harder, and produce better results when we enjoy our activity? This idea also underlies the difference between a career and a job. The former usually involves work that one chooses to pursue, often for many years or even a lifetime, as a result of personal inspiration. The latter, on the other hand, is much more likely to consist of work done on a short-term basis, out of necessity for money regardless of how one feels about the work itself. But if you could simultaneously have work that gratifies you emotionally as well as financially, wouldn't that be preferable?

Moreover, wouldn't the emotional satisfaction derived from it inspire greater commitment and thus better effort on your part? Well, this principle operates the same for youth and their work at school: Make it pleasurable, and effort will take care of itself. In other words, passion propels performance.

Remember, however, that our current educational system is based on a paradigm of efficiency, not effectiveness. This is precisely why in chapter 1 we saw Jeff Bliss, the Texas high school student, erupt in defiant frustration toward his teacher (almost twenty years after the release of *Matilda*). From the teacher's perspective, she was just doing her job as efficiently as possible by handing out photocopied worksheets. Jeff, on the other hand, found this mode of learning utterly exasperating and, consequently, lost the ability to remain silent about it any longer.

Actually, there is substantial evidence that enjoyment and learning are compatible. In fact, the former can even facilitate the latter.

Research

Speaking from her experience as a neurologist and classroom teacher, Judy Willis claims that when the fun stops, learning stops too. In her insightful article, "The Neuroscience of Joyful Education," she explains: "When students are engaged and motivated and feel minimal stress, information flows freely through the affective filter in the amygdala and they achieve higher levels of cognition, make connections, and experience 'aha' moments."[3] In other words, feeling good helps one to learn. Stress and anxiety, on the other hand, can hinder that process.

Similar reasoning can be found in "Toward More Joyful Learning" by former middle school teacher Hilary Conklin, now a professor of teacher education at DePaul University. In discussing the cultivation of twenty-first-century skills, Conklin asserts: "Play, creativity, and joy are not only absent from prominent frameworks for effective teaching, but they

Fun: Enjoyment of Learning

are also increasingly absent from young people's classrooms and lives."[4]

This concern played out in my own family when my wife and I were choosing a school for our son, who was five years old at the time. After visiting several elementary schools in our local vicinity, we narrowed the contenders down to two or three. We were a bit conflicted, however, because the school with the best reputation for academic achievement also offered the least amount of free play time—fifteen minutes daily in kindergarten. Of course, we had to ask ourselves whether we thought that school was in the best overall interest of our energetic little boy. Ultimately, this was a key factor in us deciding that it was not.

The last source of evidence I will summarize to support the idea that fun promotes learning has to do with the arts and music. Using the most rigorous research methods currently at our disposal, researchers have found that arts education and music can improve students' academic as well as nonacademic performance.[5] Their effects have been generally described as modest, however.

I should end the discussion about the relationship between the arts and academic achievement with this important point: Art and music education have value in and of themselves, not merely as methods of boosting academic achievement. Linda Nathan articulates this point quite well in her article "Joyful Learning at Scale."[6] She explains that the arts and music cultivate soft skills that are becoming increasingly valuable to individuals as the workplace and hard skills become more automated.

Unfortunately, because our system places greater value on the latter, art and music, along with recess, have all been cut significantly from the school day since the turn of the century.[7]

Ways to Make Learning Fun

We have discussed the idea that learning and having fun in school are not necessarily at odds with one another. Moreover, in the process of doing so, we reviewed considerable information supporting the contention that enjoyment not only facilitates learning but also the emotional development of youth. The remainder of this chapter offers some specific methods that anyone can use to implement fun as a strategy to promote those same ends.

Identifying activities that kids enjoy is easy. All you need to do is ask or observe. To get you started, here are some of my favorites based on the overwhelming positive reactions observed among students from my own experience as an educator:

1. Games (many can be implemented with technology tools)
2. Role-play in real-life experiences
3. Teams and small-group competition/collaboration
4. Projects or activities related to students' personal interests

Much more challenging than identifying fun activities, however, is structuring them so that kids actually learn and grow.

Here is where the business of teaching becomes both art and science. One of the best examples in schools today is technology. Cell phones, the internet, and AI (artificial intelligence) can be a blessing or a curse in the classroom, *depending on how they are used*. Given its power to engage students, I believe that educators should co-opt technology as a tool for good. Moreover, in so far as the presence of technology in our lives will only increase, students must be taught how to use it responsibly. Obviously, educators will have to participate in ongoing professional development to ensure they possess the knowledge and skill to effectively use technology for instruction.

Those who work with youth outside of regular school settings may enjoy a special advantage when it comes to using fun as a learning strategy. Precisely because their setting is not constrained by state mandates in the way that regular schools are, these youth advocates have greater freedom to exercise creativity than most educators.

Those individuals comprise a substantial portion of the Tubman Educators, which I mentioned in the book's introduction. To reiterate, these are the advocates who not only recognize the need for the emotional development of youth but also nurture it. Many work as teachers in regular schools while some work in out-of-school-time (OST) programs operated by a vast sea of community-based organizations. Still others work simply as home-schoolers. Just as the great yet humble Harriet Tubman was wanted for liberating slaves, these advocates are under siege today for liberating minds. Whereas the system focuses on making youth skillful, the Tubman Educator concentrates on making them willful. And, in doing so, they empower youth and thereby leverage their ability to excel both in school and out.

As an example, back in the day, I headed a community-based alternative education program in New Orleans called the Urban League Street Academy. The program served about fifty students who had dropped out of the regular school system. With a small staff of seven people, our aim was to help them pass the high school equivalency examination as a key step on the road to self-sufficiency. In this alternative setting, we had considerable leeway to provide instruction more creatively than in regular schools. The challenge, however, was in motivating the students to participate. To this day, I can recall how making learning fun enabled us to inspire some of the most disadvantaged youth in the city. This anecdote will illustrate methods two and four of the Fun strategy: real-life experiences and personal interests.

One week, I decided to demonstrate this approach in a mathematics class of a small group of young men. The lesson's objective was to help them understand basic concepts in multiplication and division. It occurred to me that this might be an opportunity to accomplish the learning objective—*and* have some fun in the process. Believing that switching the context from an academic setting to one of personal relevance and real-world application would both inspire student engagement and help my students grasp the mathematical operations, I arranged a field trip to a Toyota automobile dealership across the street.

Fun: Enjoyment of Learning

After a brief introduction from the textbook on the relationship between multiplication and division, we walked over to the dealership, where I had prearranged a visit. "Welcome, gentlemen," greeted the salesman. "We've been expecting you." "Thank you, sir," I replied. I then said to the students, "Okay, guys. I'd like you to find one car that you might like to own. Write down the make and model, some features, and its price. Next, what you need to do is figure out how much your monthly payment would be, depending on the amount you plan to pay up front, the down payment, and the term of the loan. For example, this red Mustang has got my attention. Yeah, it's a used car, but isn't she a beauty!" I glided my hand slowly along its side before continuing, "We see the asking price here on the windshield is $5,000. But I'm not ready to pay that much at once. So, what's my monthly payment going to be if I put down $1,000 and then have a three-year term to pay the balance? And if that monthly payment looks too high, I can calculate a lower one by extending the term to four or five years, right? Okay, guys, go to work!"

As they sputtered about the car lot, something almost magical began to happen. These young men—all dropouts, mind you—got into mathematics with enthusiasm like I had never seen before.

"Hey, y'all! Check out mah'car over here!" shouted one.

"Look at mine!" interjected another.

The car lot previously silent was now as noisy as a street festival. By the time our "class" was almost done, one of the young men looked at me with a smile of delight, and shaking his head contently, declared: "I *know* I'm going to finish school now!"

Smiling back, I thought, *Mission accomplished!*

The DAP Effect

Next, I'll give an illustration of method number three for making learning fun: teams and small-group competition/collaboration. This one took place at a regular high school in Gainesville, Florida, in an Algebra II course covering a unit on statistics. I call it "DAP," which stands for the Data Analysis Project. During my postdoctoral fellowship at the University of Florida, I studied the attitudes of students toward mathematics. I volunteered some time at a local public high school with the aim of keeping my academic studies in touch with real kids and classrooms. DAP was the result of my collaboration with a classroom teacher and her students.[8]

Consider these initial responses to our survey on how 33 percent of students felt about math: "I just don't feel urged to do it because other than basic skills, math to me is useless so my motivation to study and learn it is hard to maintain." Others suggested a change in instruction as a potential source of improving their performance in math. For example, some said they could do better in math if: "Math was taught in a different way" or "If it were more interesting and had more excitement." About one-fifth of the students agreed that math was more interesting than other classes, and only one agreed strongly with that statement (see Figure 7).

Fun: Enjoyment of Learning

**Student survey responses to the question:
"Math class is more interesting than most other classes"**

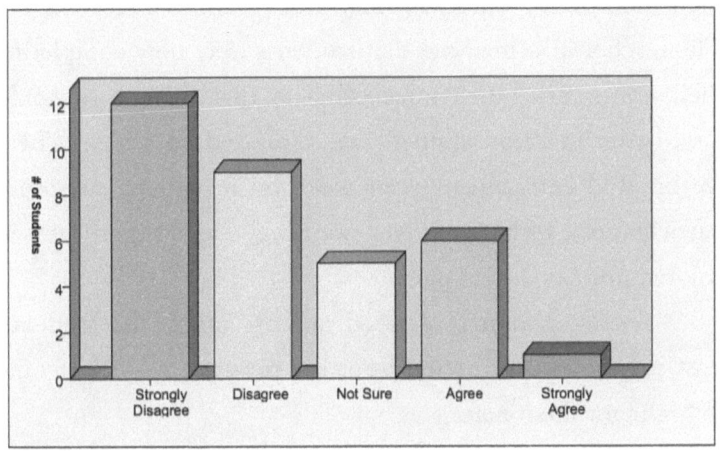

Figure 7. Olatunji and Paige, "Liking and Learning Mathematics" (2007).

But here's how we turned that situation around. Three features undergirded the Data Analysis Project: (1) engagement, (2) relevance, and (3) learning. Therefore, we used the course's five classroom periods as teams that would compete with each other, using points for homework completion and class quiz scores as yardsticks. These data were then used to generate statistical concepts for learning, such as mean, median, mode, range, quartile, and so forth. For example, rather than merely define "minimum and maximum" as the smallest and greatest values, students interpreted them meaningfully as "the lowest and highest scores for our class on last week's quiz were 35 and 95."

I noticed that the students got excited when the results of classrooms were compared in graphs using PowerPoint slides. For instance, one student interpreting the graphs declared:

"Their test scores are lower because they don't do as much of their homework." And with that declaration, the race was on! The teacher informed me that students were now completing their homework much more often so that their class would look better in these competitions projected on screen. Then, we boosted engagement even more by rewarding classroom participation with incentives seemingly as insignificant as colored notebooks and pens.

We were absolutely amazed at how much the students' post-survey results differed from the pre-survey, so I'm going to highlight them here:

- 73 percent said that the project helped them to understand statistics.
- 85 percent agreed that the project helped them to see the utility of mathematics.
- 90 percent agreed that using their own data was an effective teaching strategy.
- 94 percent said that they liked the Data Analysis Project.

And following are some of their most notable comments:

- "People are more interested in the things they do, so it's better to look at your own data than someone else's."
- "It helped me realize how important homework was and how much doing homework and studying can improve your grade."

- "It puts everything into a visual format that makes it easier to understand."
- "Yes, it is a very good way to learn math."

Thus, by making math more meaningful and enjoyable, the project promoted student engagement as well as learning.

Not long ago, I applied the personal interests method with my young son to help him understand mathematical concepts such as place value and quantity in order to read and compare numbers. While my seventeen-year-old students were motivated by cars, my seven-year-old was turned on by ships. I won't describe the whole story, but the approach was basically the same. Once I told him I wanted to play a numbers game that involved the legendary RMS *Titanic*, he was sold! And according to his teacher, his math skills improved. Most importantly, nothing gave me more satisfaction than seeing the smile on his face as he proudly expressed joy over his ability to read and understand numbers.

In closing, here's a tip that you can use in any classroom setting or grade level. I recommend that you survey your students, preferably at the beginning of the school year. You want to learn about their interests, what they like, and what motivates them. If you don't have many students, then you could easily survey them in a small-group discussion activity. If the group is larger, however, I recommend you survey them with an online tool or with pen and paper. That information is now the fodder you can use the rest of the year to fuel fun activities. Moreover, doing so will also help you to build supportive relationships with students, as they will see that you value their interests. So, don't just store that information and forget about it. Use it to push your students' motivational buttons until they no longer need you to. You may download a free copy of my student interest survey at: DrOinspires.com.

By now it should be clear: Fun is an instructional strategy that works with students regardless of age or subject area. In the next chapter, we'll explore the second powerful feature of the FACES framework: Affirmation.

Fun: Enjoyment of Learning

AUTHOR'S KEY POINTS

1. In conventional schooling, having fun and learning are a contradiction in terms.
2. There is substantial research demonstrating that the former can promote the latter.
3. Use games, role-play, team activities, the personal interests of students, and technology responsibly to make learning enjoyable as well as educational.

MY KEY REFLECTIONS

1. What in this chapter left the biggest impression on me?

2. What personal experiences, if any, did this chapter bring to mind?

3. What action might I or others take based on what I've learned?

CHAPTER 7

Affirmation: "I Like It When You Call Me Teresita!"

Our first job as teachers is to make sure that we learn our students . . . showing respect for their culture and affirming their worthiness to receive the best education possible.

—James E. Ford, founder, Be More Foundation

We have begun building a new paradigm for education, first by exploring why the learning process itself should and can be enjoyable for kids. Now, the second feature of the FACES framework focuses on a need essential for youth success: Affirmation. As we shall see, affirmation is indeed a powerful element, one that promotes the overall well-being of youth and not only their academic achievement.

According to *Merriam-Webster*, to affirm is to validate or to confirm. Examining the word's etymology, one finds its Middle English predecessor *affermen*, which meant to fix firmly or to make steadfast. It is easy to see the connection therefore between the modern English word and its Latin root *affirmare*, which means to strengthen or to fortify.[1]

Turning again to his beautiful book on words, Kevin Hall asserts, "When you are validated, you are given strength, power, and authority."[2] In the FACES framework, this is precisely what Affirmation means. When we affirm youth, we validate them; we give them strength, power, and authority.

Validation makes us firm emotionally and spiritually by enhancing our self-esteem. The message one receives when validated is that "you are worthy, you are important, you matter." In light of the negative messages perpetuated today through social media, it is particularly important that young people receive validation from caring adults.

Looking further into *Merriam-Webster*'s definition, we find that "affirm implies conviction based on evidence, experience, or faith." Let's now bridge this understanding of the word with the crucial role educators play in affirming students. In doing so, we'll delve into how an educator's beliefs influence the affirmation process and why this holds tremendous significance in education.

Consider, for example, what this definition might mean for students on the first day of school when a teacher has no prior evidence or experience with them. Validating a student in advance can only stem from a deep belief on the part of the teacher that the student is indeed worthy.

Now, if an educator views the youth in her class from the conventional education paradigm where students are like empty bottles waiting to be filled according to their innate abilities, then having such faith is in doubt. On the other hand, if the educator sees her students as already gifted, in keeping with the new paradigm proposed in chapter 5, then having such faith is a given. Thus, I urge every parent to seriously consider who might be charged with their child's education, for educators have the power to validate their students—or not. The significance of this point will become clearer as this chapter proceeds. In addition to summarizing what I consider the most relevant research, we'll review some actual examples of why affirmation is a critical part of youth success. Last, we'll learn some specific ways to affirm young learners.

Research

Does any research support the idea that affirming students matters? You bet. Most of that work appears to pertain to the university level after the 1960s, as student enrollment at college campuses became increasingly diverse. Laura I. Rendón, professor emerita at the University of Texas–San Antonio, has developed a theory of validation as a way of helping first-generation college students from low-income families to succeed. According to Rendón:

Validation helped these kinds of students to acquire a confident, motivating, "I can do it" attitude, believe in their inherent capacity to learn, become excited about learning, feel a part of the learning community, and feel cared about as a person, not just a student.[3]

If you think about it, this theory seems to encompass the same three elements that I discussed under self-determination theory. Autonomy is present as students become confident and motivated. Competence is nurtured as they develop belief in their inherent capacity to learn. Students experience relatedness or a sense of belonging as they come to feel a part of the learning community. And remember: the founders of self-determination theory considered it to be based on the psychological needs of every human being. Consequently, although validation theory has been used primarily to help economically disadvantaged students, I would argue that validation is something we all need. In fact, Oprah Winfrey underscored the same in her 2013 commencement speech at Harvard University, in which she, reflecting on a previous interview with superstar Beyoncé, asserted that even "Beyoncé and all of her Beyoncéness" expressed the need for validation.[4]

When you consider not only what it means to be validated but also its power, it's easy to grasp the inherent value of gender- and ethnicity-based educational institutions. It seems fair to say that, in general, students who attend women-only institutions, historically Black colleges and universities (HBCUs), or Hispanic-serving institutions (HSIs) are more likely to experience a learning environment that affirms them than they would at a traditional school. I can personally attest to this through my experience as a former professor at Dillard University, an HBCU in New Orleans. There, I taught the Foundations of Education course one year after teaching Sociology 101 at Tulane University, where students from many of the nation's elite families are found. I could easily write a chapter, if not an entire book, on how different these institutions were in terms of affirmation, not merely for students but also for me as an instructor.

Insofar as validation is a human need, its value applies to students at all levels of the education ladder. Laura Huang provides one excellent example in her highly acclaimed book *Edge: Turning Adversity into Advantage*.[5] A history teacher had students write down a personal goal on an index card, which he then read to the class. One student wrote: "My goal is to teach everyone in this class how to spell Zimbabwe," to which the teacher replied, "Zimbabwe . . . I'll make sure you all know how that country is spelled, *and* where it is!" Another wrote: "My goal is to make the football team." "Yup, you've got a great football arm—I think you'll make it," responded the teacher.

A pretty good job affirming students, don't you think?

But Huang then wrote about the experience of Cerelina, her thirteen-year-old mentee, whom she accompanied on the first day of high school. Unfortunately, Cerelina's case was heartbreaking.

Reacting to her card which read, "'My goal for high school is to study hard and be awarded a Rhodes Scholarship to study at Oxford University,'" the teacher chuckled before remarking: "'Ambitious,' and then under his breath, 'Let's not get our hopes up.'" The girl's face, according to Huang, was "burning with embarrassment." Yet worse, the impact of the teacher's words on that day apparently had long-lasting, negative effects.

Consider this excerpt from Huang's book:

> I pulled her aside after class and told her Oxford was a wonderful goal—that she could do it, and that with hard work and perseverance, nothing could stop her. But years later . . . she fell far short, getting pregnant and dropping out of school . . . On the day she dropped out . . . she brought up that index card from her first day of high school. She told me, "Hard work doesn't get people like me into Oxford. Hard work doesn't work that way for me."[6]

My dear youth advocate, doesn't this story substantiate, as I asserted earlier, that educators have the power to validate their students—or not? Does it not demonstrate why affirmation is an important part of the educational process? And does it not confirm once more how real and harmful the problem of alienation from school can be?

With that in mind, then, I urge parents to take care of the school environments in which you place your child. And as their primary advocate, I encourage you to make it a point to have those daily conversations with them about school as well as any other activities that consume a part of their day or week. You want to make sure that they are being supported and not injured by teachers, peers, or the learning environment in any way.

"I Like It When You Call Me Teresita!"

I'll never forget an experience I had early on in my career. It took place in Texas at a national conference for educational policymakers and practitioners concerned about the challenges confronting disadvantaged youth. I attended as assistant director of the Clearinghouse on Urban Education, then located at Teachers College, Columbia University in New York City. Although I can remember neither the title of the session nor the full name of the presenter, something happened in that room that stayed with me for the rest of my life. The presenter, a Mexican American woman whom I'll simply call "Dr. Teresa," gave a powerful lesson that day on the importance of affirming youth.

At the start of her presentation, Dr. Teresa sat perched upon a stool at the front of the room. This kindled curiosity because conference presenters usually sit behind a podium or a desk. *What is she going to do?* I wondered. Maybe thirty-something years old, average in height and size, and dressed in professional attire, she gave no clue. Then, when confident that most who planned to attend the session had arrived, she began her presentation.

With sparkling eyes, upright shoulders and chest, and a smile that glowed like a crescent moon in the night sky, exuding all the excitement typical of a five-year-old child, she startled the audience:

"*Hola! Me llamo* Teresa Espinosa Gonzales, but everybody calls me Teresita!"

Switching between English and Spanish with a notable accent, Dr. Teresa recounted her experience as an immigrant child to the United States from Mexico. There, perched upon that stool for roughly forty-five minutes, she dramatically portrayed her feelings as she progressed through the school system from kindergarten to high school, when she dropped out in the ninth grade. After blurting out her name, Dr. Teresa continued her monologue, depicting her kindergarten teacher's response.

"Welcome to the United States! I'm so excited you're here. One of the first things we'll have to do, however, is get that name straight. Your name is no longer Teresita. Now it's Terry."

Dr. Teresa gently placed her hand underneath her chin, elevating it slightly. Portraying her teacher, she then pronounced her name in English, ever so slowly stretching out each letter, exaggerating the movements of her jaw, mouth, and lips in the process.

"Can you say it? Te-e-r-r-y."

Up until that time in my life, if you had asked me what I had in common with a Hispanic woman, a "Latina," I might have facetiously replied, "*Nada.*" Yet, there I sat captivated by her words and emotions. The longer she went on with her story,

Affirmation: "I Like It When You Call Me Teresita!"

the clearer it became to me that her experience was similar to my own as an African American, or a "person of color" in the United States.

"Call me *Teresita, por favor*. My name is Teresita. I like it when you call me Teresita."

Dr. Teresa continued her presentation without interruption. She progressed through a few years in elementary school. This time she described a similar interaction on the playground with a male physical education instructor.

"You've gotta catch that ball, Terry. You can do it," he encouraged.

To which, with her Spanish accent, she replied: "My name is Teresita. *Please* call me Teresita. I like it when people call me Teresita." I'd be willing to bet that I wasn't the only one who felt a tone of annoyance, if not frustration, in Dr. Teresa's voice, a tone that clearly was absent when she first encountered this situation in kindergarten.

Dr. Teresa then recounted her instructor's admonishment as he made eye-to-eye contact with her after a curt chuckle: "Well, that might have been your name in Mexico, but you're in the US of A now. Here your name is Terry. You can say that, can't you? Te-e-rry."

Just as she did when portraying the first experience, Dr. Teresa again exaggerated the pronunciation of her name in English. This time, however, she also released a sigh that seemed to intensify her feeling of annoyance into one of desperation.

There I sat, not merely entertained but also mesmerized as her monologue continued, chronicling such experiences from elementary to middle school. I believe it was during this portion of her presentation that I began to feel some of my own painful experiences in education resurfacing to consciousness. Painful because just as with Dr. Teresa, those experiences had assaulted rather than affirmed my identity in some way. Her words began to rekindle feelings of anger, embarrassment, and alienation from my high school years.

As I sat listening to the story of "Teresita," I began to imagine myself, about ten years prior, as the only Black student in my American literature class in the eleventh grade. It was the one and only time that I recall any mention of African Americans by my instructors during my three-year tenure at the school. And of all the topics and authors that could have been introduced—as much for my sake as for my White upper-middle-class peers—the teacher made reference to a tale by Ernest Hemingway about a Black woman who enjoyed being a prostitute. *That* was pretty much the extent of "diversity and inclusion" in my day. The message implied, of course, was that African Americans had made no contributions to American literature worthy of inclusion in the school's curriculum.

As my awareness gradually returned to Dr. Teresa's presentation, she now was recounting her first year in high school, ninth grade. The tone of her voice and the posture of her body told the story more powerfully than any words could. The sparkling fire with which she had introduced herself as a kindergarten student was now extinguished. On the stool she sat slouched over and with her face covered completely

Affirmation: "I Like It When You Call Me Teresita!"

by apathy, reminding me, in fact, of the ninth graders I had taught in New York City. Role-playing her response to a teacher urging her to participate in class, Teresita just whined and complained: "I don't know what I'm gonna do today. I just don't feel like doing anything... You know what? Maybe school just isn't for me."

Dr. Teresa ended her story about dropping out of high school in a most unconventional fashion. She got off her stool and walked straight out of the room. We, the audience, waited patiently for her return, anticipating a much-needed opportunity for some Q&A. However... Dr. Teresa never returned.

I was absolutely flabbergasted! And yet, I believe I had understood her message perfectly. "Touché, Dr. Teresa," I said to myself, nodding my head with a smile on my face. Seeking more information, I read in the conference program that despite dropping out of high school, she later reenrolled. Not only did she graduate, but she went on to finish college and eventually earned a doctorate. Unsurprisingly, all of those achievements, according to her bio, were largely inspired by the encouragement and guidance from an adult woman, another Latina who mentored her.

If I could meet her today, I'm sure that Dr. Teresa would say that her mentor gave her not only guidance and encouragement, but also affirmation. I'm sure she'd agree that the mentor validated her not only as a Mexican American but also as a person. Teresita's mentor believed in her, which in turn helped Teresita to believe in herself. And yes, I'm sure she would also say that it made all the difference in the world to have someone who understood how much it meant whenever she said, "I like it when you call me Teresita!"

And so, my dear youth advocate, now that we have discussed the meaning and importance of affirmation, I leave you with this list of nine ways that you can do so for the young people in your life. The list (edited by the author) is taken directly from experiences identified by Rendón in her research on validating college students,[7] which I find applies to younger students as well:

1. Take the time to learn and refer to them by name.
2. Give students opportunities to witness themselves as successful learners.
3. Ensure that the curriculum reflects students' backgrounds.
4. Share knowledge with students and become partners in learning.
5. Verbally support youth, for example: "You can do this!" (Verbal support also includes expressing appreciation for their backgrounds, interests, and aspirations).
6. Take the time to help students select courses and plan their futures.
7. Support youth in their quest to graduate from school.
8. Encourage students to support each other.
9. Mentor students.

Affirmation: "I Like It When You Call Me Teresita!"

The Promise

Earth, Wind & Fire used to sing a jubilant song about dancing in September. The song ushered in my first year as a college student at Harvard University in the fall of 1978. In politics, less than three months prior to my arrival, the U.S. Supreme Court had ruled that race could be used as a factor in college admissions. Jimmy Carter was president, and to his credit, he brokered a peace agreement that year between Israelis and Palestinians. Many of the protests that would take place on campus, however, had to do with South Africa's apartheid and Nelson Mandela, who had already been imprisoned for fifteen years by the time my studies began. Eulogized worldwide today for his transformative leadership, he was then regarded as a terrorist by many, including the U.S. government.[8]

The university's intellectual milieu was like nothing I had ever experienced before—nor since, I might add. The size of my class was roughly 1,500 students. Rather than fill those slots with a homogeneous group of applicants whose SAT scores were perfect, the university opted for a heterogeneous student body composed of young men and women from all over the world, representing all racial and ethnic backgrounds and social classes, which entailed a broad range of college admissions test scores. Thus, the social environment was itself a unique asset for learning from the perspectives of others, outside as well as inside the classroom.

Complementing the diversity of my talented peers was the immensity of the university's tremendous resources, especially its libraries. And whereas the faculty is typically regarded as a school's greatest resource, undergraduate students at Harvard had limited contact with professors. Most of their time was devoted to research and students at the graduate level. I was fortunate enough, however, to develop a close relationship with one of them during my tenure.

The Peril

Not only was I prepared academically, but I was also highly motivated personally to pursue my college education. And although uncertain about what I wanted to do with my life, I was convinced that this was an investment in my future that would pay off no matter what direction I eventually chose. On the far side of opportunity, however, lies challenge, the likes of which in my case had little to do with intellect. In time, it would become clear that in order to graduate, I would need far more than a solid academic preparation.

I had gotten off to a fair start as measured by my grades at the end of the first semester. According to my academic advisor, my grade point average was typical for an incoming freshman. As the year progressed, however, my grades declined like a submarine diving beneath the surface of the sea. In fact, over my first two years at Harvard, I struggled academically to keep my head above water. It has been said in college

Affirmation: "I Like It When You Call Me Teresita!"

admissions that if they let you in, it means they believe you can do the work. What then was my problem?

Now, it would be disingenuous of me if I attributed my problem solely to schooling. After all, it's important to remember that first and foremost, each of us is a human being. To be perfectly honest, I should stress that my underperformance was affected severely by personal factors. The greatest among them was simply adolescence. At least in the Western world, this is the phase in life when one transitions from childhood to adulthood. The stage is naturally turbulent psychologically and oftentimes painful emotionally.

In my particular case, I was struggling internally with questions about life from the perspective of my religious fundamentalist upbringing. Going back and forth between the communities of faith in New Orleans and Swarthmore had caused me to question the inconsistencies that I observed between the two. Now the community in Cambridge exacerbated the situation. During one of my trips home, for example, one of my faith teachers declared: "You shouldn't have gone away to that school; you used to be a lot more humble. Now you question everything!"

She was right. In fact, in hindsight I now can see that I was constantly in a state of questioning my own paradigm and assumptions about life. When I left New Orleans at age fifteen, I saw life simply as black and white, in terms of morality. Right and wrong were as clear and distinct as day and night. In contrast, by age eighteen, I had been forced to struggle with different paradigms. No longer did morality seem to be merely a black-and-white affair, but instead a spectrum comprised of infinite shades of gray, one for each person on the planet.

Thus, as an adolescent, I was engaged in exactly the type of self-examination encouraged by Stephen Covey (see chapter 5), only my doing so was prompted by direct encounters with the diverse perspectives of others rather than by reading books. Importantly, other points of view not only helped me to develop my own—they also enhanced it. With the ability to see beyond the limits of my own perspective, I was better able to understand others and perhaps build mutually beneficial relationships with them as well.

Furthermore, prior to leaving Swarthmore, I had been bitten by the love bug. I had formed a deep emotional bond with a girl at the college, which remained intact until my first semester. The long distance between us was a torture, and I was devastated when she eventually broke up with me.

Heaped on top of all that, I was struggling to figure out how to cope with racism. The absence of Black people in my high school's curriculum, along with reading *The Autobiography of Malcolm X* during my senior year, left me with feelings of anger, feelings I did not know quite what to do with. As a result, and perhaps to my own detriment, I distanced myself from Whites and anything European.

Harvard, in its own way, kindled the flames of my adolescent distress. I was a member of a racial and ethnic minority group from a working-class background attending a school that, until recently, had been educating only the nation's elite

Affirmation: "I Like It When You Call Me Teresita!"

for centuries. It should come as no surprise that I might be a prime candidate for experiencing alienation both socially and culturally. Such alienation, in turn, negatively impacted my ability to study.

Consider, for example, the troublesome messages that might be communicated to all students—regardless of their race—by a sculpture in Adams House, one of the university's dormitories. The sculpture displayed three human figures. One depicted an African man holding a club, another portrayed what appeared to be a native or indigenous person with a ring in his nose and holding a ball, and another showed a European man holding an open book. In the context of contemporary history, I assume that the harmful implications of such "artwork" are obvious. That the university has hidden or removed the sculpture, to my understanding, underscores as much. The point, however, is one that should not be missed: This example illustrates how racism is woven into American institutions and threatens the well-being of all.

The social environment itself was thus a subtle yet significant force that influenced my emotional state. Sadly, far too often I felt like a "piece in" rather than a "part of" the Harvard community.

It wasn't long before all of these forces took their toll on me emotionally and then academically. I sank into depression. I had lost the clarity and direction that religion, the North Star of my life, had provided up until that time. Thus, by the spring of my first year, it was as if I were sailing on a ship through the mysterious Bermuda Triangle where none of the navigation instruments, especially the compass, functioned properly. I felt totally submerged in confusion about life to the point that studying became something I did only in my spare time, which of course had its consequences.

On one of those days, while "chillin'" in the dorm with a small group of friends (my favorite activity, which actually served as a kind of survival mechanism), I received a telephone call from the university administration. In a sympathetic tone, the academic advisor on the other end informed me that due to my low grades, I would be placed on academic probation. The message was dreadful yet unsurprising.

As this hurricane of personal confusion persisted, my mental health reached rock bottom. It got to the point where I even attempted suicide. I disclosed some of my feelings to an academic advisor who recommended that I seek counseling at the university health center. My initial session ended up being my last, however, as the interaction with the health professional felt too clinical and impersonal, without any sense of human connection. I believe the one thing that pushed me from tipping over the edge completely was fear of the pain that killing myself might cause my mother. Although I doubt that she could ever imagine my struggles, the tenderness of her voice assuaged my despair, as only a mother's voice could. In occasional telephone calls, I had shared that I was not happy. Then, one day, whether an advisor or a fellow student I do not remember, another confidant of mine suggested I meet with the university chaplain; I did. And that's when things began to turn around.

Affirmation: "I Like It When You Call Me Teresita!"

The Protection

Ironically, despite excellent preparation in high school specifically designed to improve my chances of succeeding in college, I was failing academically. My underperformance, however, was the symptom of factors other than academic skills. Further, as an adolescent, I had yet to develop the maturity or ability to cope effectively with those factors. Consequently, I do not pretend to blame Harvard University for all my woes. My experience would probably have been similar at any selective and predominantly White institution in the United States.

Question: Had I not thrived in a similar environment for three years prior? Absolutely. But the social supports that sustained me had now been largely removed. Whereas the ABC scholarship program and community intentionally—though imperfectly—aimed to support my success, the experience in Cambridge was much closer to the real world. You either learned to swim, or sink. And I, admittedly, was drowning.

During the second semester of my freshman year, I met University Chaplain and Professor Peter J. Gomes (now deceased) at his office in the campus chapel. Although a confidant had recommended him, I was nonetheless apprehensive. Almost immediately after meeting Gomes, however, I began to feel at ease. His appearance alone reminded me that I was at Harvard, yet he came across as warm, personable, and extremely well spoken. There he sat, reclined snugly in an elaborate, upholstered wooden chair behind a large desk, arms resting over his belly with hands joined and fingers interlaced. His smile and relaxed demeanor made me feel the same.

"So, how can I help you, young man?"

I explained my situation as best I could, curious to see what he might make of it. That he was a cleric gave me hope that he might appreciate the conflict and confusion I was experiencing over faith. In short, I could not understand how it was possible for the "believers" I knew in different places to interpret the Bible differently. Should the meaning of God's Word vary by location? And as far as some believers were concerned, including those in my family, there was absolutely no room for questioning the Word of God. After listening attentively for a while, he looked at me through his professorial spectacles and replied in a tone of voice that was as soothing as it was sage-like: "So by questioning your faith, it's as if you've gone to Harvard and thus gone to hell."

"Y-yess!" I blurted. I was stunned! In a single sentence, he had summarized my dilemma. In that moment, for me, it was as though dark clouds that covered the sky had finally parted, giving way to the sun's radiant light. For the rest of our meeting, I listened closely. Encouragingly, he bridged the gap in years between us by sharing some of his personal story with me about similar challenges he faced as a young man. By the time our conversation ended, for the first time in a long time, I felt that someone understood me. In a word, I felt validated.

From then on, I met regularly with Rev. Gomes, and I remained enlightened by whatever he had to say. On one of those occasions, he explained: "You see, what you are doing is filtering the Word through your experience." *What a brilliant way of putting it*, I thought. His words, in fact, bring to

Affirmation: "I Like It When You Call Me Teresita!"

mind a quote on a poster I had displayed proudly in my dorm room, reflecting my gradual reconstitution. It read: "A ship in a harbor is safe—but that's not what ships are built for." As a younger adolescent, I never had to think much about morality; it was always laid out for me in black and white on pages of scripture. As an older adolescent, however, the world around me demanded that I learn how to think for myself to chart my course through life. Thus, as a result of my conversations with Rev. Gomes, I slowly began to heal emotionally. I was on my way to becoming my own person, a process of change that would continue well into the next two years.

Those conversations also primed me for a future event that bolstered my recovery and fortified my resilience. An African American couple, husband and wife, returned ten years later as alumni to speak with Black students. What struck me as particularly useful in their presentation was the idea that we could improve our academic performance by recognizing and believing in our inner strengths, regardless of whatever was going on in the social environment around us. Their affirmation helped me to become more proactive, which in turn encouraged me to spend a semester abroad in Spain. And by the time I graduated, I had emerged as my own person from the turbulent years of adolescence to the promise of young adulthood.

Years later, at my twenty-fifth reunion, I shared with Rev. Gomes that those meetings may well have saved my life. His ability to listen, empathize, and clarify gave me personal validation. He had helped me to find my way. And the way that I eventually found to move forward, however imperfect, was based upon my own experiences and convictions, rather than someone else's. "Thus," I said to him with a hearty hug and smile, "I will forever be grateful for the peace and calm I found as an undergraduate at *Port Peter Gomes*."

Enjoying a moment with my former mentor, Rev. Peter J. Gomes, at Harvard University in June of 2007.

As a final reflection, I think it is important to stress my belief that my experience was not unique to me on account of my race or personal background. I would not be surprised to find similar stories among the international students (those who immigrate to the United States) or even among White American students who come from communities where going to college is not the norm. In each case, aside from whatever personal circumstances might exist, living in a culture different from one's own presents additional challenges to one's success. And while I firmly believe that institutions should do their part to promote positive learning environments, I believe just as strongly that individual students must assume personal responsibility for their own well-being and success. Thus, I have written this book to help advocates achieve either of these ends or both.

AUTHOR'S KEY POINTS

1. Under the FACES framework for a new educational paradigm, to affirm youth is to validate them.
2. Validating students sends the message that they are valued for who they are and that they add value to the community.
3. Validate students by building positive relationships with them and creating learning environments that support them personally as well as academically.

MY KEY REFLECTIONS

1. What in this chapter left the biggest impression on me?

2. What personal experiences, if any, did this chapter bring to mind?

3. What action might I or others take based on what I've learned?

CHAPTER 8

Challenge: Using Connection and Direction

We cannot become what we need to be by remaining what we are.

—Max De Pree, American business leader and writer

We have arrived at one of the most important chapters in this work, which espouses a perspective that many would never imagine this book to include. Up to now, I have placed a great deal of emphasis on the need for making education more user-friendly, if you will, for students by making schooling a more enjoyable experience. Now, however, I declare that anyone who thinks this work is simply a "kumbaya" book denying the value of hard work clearly hasn't read this chapter. In the FACES framework, Challenge, as we shall see, walks hand in hand with Affirmation. Here is where the role of rigor comes into play, especially for students who some believe are incapable of handling it. Challenge is about keeping the nose to the grindstone. Importantly, it is also where we finish the discussion about the word passion—and thus why I proclaim: *Passion propels performance!*

When speaking of Challenge within the FACES framework, I use the word in the sense of pushing or encouraging youth to do more and to become more. You, as an adult, can see both a young person's potential as well as the obstacles to their success much more clearly than they can. Consequently, as an advocate, you are the one who should challenge them to achieve more than they know or believe is possible.

The adult advocate is to the adolescent what the sports coach is to the athlete. The knowledge gained through years of experience is what makes the coach so valuable to the athlete. No matter how good the latter's skill and talent, the former's superior insight directs and transforms them into success. Therein lies the truth behind the Hausa (West African) proverb: *Strategy is better than strength.* Therefore, if we want our young people to make the most of themselves, we must challenge them! Just as rigorous training is essential for developing the potential of every athlete, so is it necessary as well for developing the knowledge, skills, and perspectives of every adolescent. Rigor, in fact, is precisely what student Jeff Bliss, in chapter 1, was craving.[1]

Challenge: Using Connection and Direction

In education, the concept of challenge is closely related to the idea of "holding high expectations" for student achievement. A plethora of research supports the idea that when educators communicate high expectations, their students excel. As the seminal German philosopher Goethe once wrote: "Treat a man as he is, and that is what he remains. Treat a man as he can be, and that is what he becomes."[2]

Something about human beings helps us to excel, to defy the odds whenever we feel the persistent presence of encouragement from another.

Using Connection and Direction to Make Youth Thrive

So how does one go about challenging youth? What do you do to provide the guidance they typically don't even know they need? Do you give them a written list of steps to follow? Do you tell them again and again that they'll be sorry one day for not listening to the voice of experience? I think not. The strategy for challenging youth I give you in this chapter is what I call "Connection and Direction." Connection refers to the caring relationships we cultivate with youth to give them the guidance they need to achieve success, to thrive.

Connection and Direction need a mechanism, however, to leverage their effects. Otherwise, youth are likely to regard one's earnest efforts to challenge them as yet another unnecessary and unwelcomed adult imposition. The solution is to combine Challenge with Affirmation. In fact, think of these two features of the FACES framework as opposite sides of the same coin. Affirmation and Challenge are the keys to building the relationships that make youth receptive to the guidance they need from you as their advocate, mentor, and teacher. Two excellent examples follow in the pages ahead.

Aside from this two-pronged approach, we must understand the meaning of the word *passion* if we are going to challenge youth effectively. Thus far, I have talked about passion only in terms of pleasure and emotional fulfillment in our activities as human beings. There is, however, another side to the coin as well.

In chapter 5, A New Paradigm for Education, I discussed how Kevin Hall, author of *Aspire*, explained that from its origin, enthusiasm means "God within."[3] This meaning embodies the fervor and desire akin to passion itself. In chapter 6, we explored how the conventional educational process can be enhanced and transformed by incorporating fun or enjoyment of learning. Now it is time to take our understanding up yet another notch by examining the origin of the word *passion*. In doing so, once again I quote Hall's mentor, Professor Watkins, who he referred to as the Master of Words:

> The word "*passion*" first surfaced in the twelfth century. Coined by Christian scholars, it means *to suffer*. In its purest sense it describes the "willing suffering of Christ." . . . Then he revealed a link between suffering, or passion, and sacrifice. "The word 'sacrifice' comes from the Latin

'*sacra*,' which means sacred, and 'fice,' which means *to* perform. To sacrifice is to perform the sacred." . . . Even though it has become popular to define passion as deep or romantic love, the real meaning is *being willing to suffer for what you love*. When we discover what we are willing to pay a price for, we discover our life's mission and purpose.[4]

These insights combined with my own lead to an inevitable conclusion: Pleasure and pain are but opposite sides to the coin of passion. Having said as much, you the youth advocate should now have a clear understanding of what's ahead. To bring out the best in the youth under your care, you must do more than affirm them. It is also your job to challenge them. And in doing so, you must build supportive relationships as the bridge for providing rigor.

Two Exemplary Tubman Educators

Following are two exemplary models of what it means in the FACES framework to challenge youth. Both, in fact, epitomize the Tubman Educator, a concept I introduced in the introduction. The following two teachers worked during roughly the same time period but in different school systems. Most notably, both worked with students who came from communities overwhelmed by poverty, crime, and a history of low academic achievement. One stressed literacy and the other mathematics.

Don't Let School Get in the Way of Education

And although both are deceased, their legacies remain ever so relevant to education today. After reading their stories, you will have no doubt that we can and must challenge youth with Connection and Direction, with relationship and rigor.

To circumvent the obstacles and frustration she had experienced as a teacher in the public school system of Chicago, Marva Collins opened the doors of Westside Preparatory School in 1975. Now as principal of her own elementary school, she was able to freely implement the educational practices she thought best for her students. Despite the fact that most of her students came from one of the city's worst neighborhoods, Collins lowered neither her standards nor her expectations.

With an unusual combination of academic rigor and personal affirmation, she challenged students in ways they could never have imagined. Consider the following excerpts from her book, *Marva Collins' Way*: "The first thing we are going to do in here, children, is an awful lot of believing in ourselves."[5] Notice that this outstanding teacher began instruction not by introducing academic subject matter, but instead by fortifying the *ultimate subject*: the student. By reinforcing the students' own sense of self-worth, she primes them for the rigorous work ahead, as demonstrated here: "In September my second-graders had started out with the first book in the [curriculum] series; in June they finished up in the middle of the fifth-grade reader. They knew of Aristotle, Aesop, Tolstoy, Shakespeare, Poe, Frost, and Dickinson."[6]

Have you registered the significance of what you just read? Collins worked with students who came to her with educational deficits, those far behind their peers. But within a single year, many if not most were reading above grade level. Extraordinary! Remarkably, she was able to produce such results consistently, year after year, to the point where there was a waiting list of parents to enroll their children in Westside Prep. Eventually, Collins's reputation was so outstanding that she was offered the post of Secretary of Education by two U.S. presidents.[7]

Particularly noteworthy is how Collins exemplified the true spirit of Harriet Tubman. Explaining the difficulty she experienced teaching in the regular school system, she recounts: "I had to sneak in the lessons on Shakespeare because they were never included in the curriculum prescribed by the Board of Education. Many educators and textbook publishers seemed to think that children should not be reading Shakespeare or, for that matter, any other great works of literature."[8] As you can see, therefore, in light of the book banning taking place across the country today, youth advocates in community-based organizations can help to ensure, as did Marva Collins, that the educational needs of students are met.

Even more significant than enriching the curriculum, however, was how Collins enriched her students' mentality by teaching personal responsibility. "No one is going to hand you anything on a platter, not in this classroom. Not in this life," she once stressed to her students. "You determine what you will be."[9]

Unfortunately, as any Tubman Educator should expect, many persons, including some of her colleagues, did not celebrate her accomplishments. Instead of praising her student achievement, they completely denied it. One of the most notable was Dr. Charles Murray, also one of the co-authors of the controversial book *The Bell Curve: Intelligence and Class Structure in American Life*. Murray, an expert, if not an authority on the measurement of IQ, dismissed the remarkable academic achievement of students at Westside Prep, which directly contradicted the ideas in his book. According to journalist Morley Safer, Murray described the highly acclaimed results of Collins and her students in his book as "too good to be true."[10] In his featured story on *60 Minutes*, however, Safer went on to share seemingly incontrovertible evidence of the students' achievement, revealed in actual interviews with them years later as successful adults.

Our second Tubman Educator worked at the other end of the K-12 educational spectrum, but with effects every bit as remarkable. During the 1980s, Jaime Escalante took student achievement from the lowest to highest levels as a mathematics teacher at Garfield High School in the Los Angeles public schools. His subject: calculus.

Many of us have come to believe in the myth that only those with above-average intelligence can master math. After all, compared to other subjects, math instruction relies much more on the use of numbers and symbols rather than words. Students often experience math as a sort of foreign language for communicating abstract (and seemingly useless) ideas. Thus, anyone who can grasp and apply that language easier or faster than most is often viewed as someone with innately high intelligence. Whether or not this is true, what is more important is the fact that *virtually anyone* can learn and excel in math, given adequate support and instruction. The work of Jaime Escalante makes this point exceptionally clear.

In Escalante's first few years at Garfield High, with an enrollment of about 3,300 students, the school had more students participating in gangs than in upper math courses. About 90 percent of the students did not take math at all or took only a basic course below algebra. Ninety-eight percent of the studentship was Hispanic, with nearly half categorized as LEP (limited English proficient). From this unlikely pool, Escalante gleaned eighteen students as candidates for the Advanced Placement (AP) calculus examination, a national standardized test frequently used in assessing applicants for college admissions.[11] To make a long story short, all eighteen passed the examination not once but twice. Because the Educational Testing Service, which administered the test, accused the students of cheating the first time, they were required to retake the exam. Escalante's program grew each year and peaked in 1987 with eighty-five students passing the AP calculus exam. As a result, Garfield High became one of the highest-performing schools in the nation, in terms of the exam. And Escalante became a hero.

How on earth did he and his students accomplish this? Escalante summarized their success with one word (in Spanish): "*Ganas!*" The meaning of this word certainly would not be surprising, if you have paid attention to this book. After writing "GANAS" [DESIRE] on the chalkboard, Escalante explained to his students, "Ganas means determination, discipline, hard work. We need students with ganas."[12]

Escalante's methods comprised some powerful ingredients. Without a doubt, the high expectations that Escalante consistently communicated to his students were crucial to his success. Until he created a calculus program at the school, *there was none.* His videos on YouTube as well as the movie about him, *Stand and Deliver,* suggest that the first feature of the FACES framework, Fun, was also one of his strategies, as he would wear costumes and tell jokes to capture the attention of students. And to counter the effects of society's negative stereotypes of Hispanic culture, which he undoubtedly recognized as a threat to his students' self-esteem, Escalante skillfully weaved affirming facts into his instruction. As depicted in *Stand and Deliver,* for example, once while teaching, he asserted that the Mayans—who might be considered culturally as their Central American ancestors—had developed the mathematical concept of zero, while the Greeks and Romans had none at all.[13] And in no small measure, Escalante relentlessly insisted that students take personal responsibility for their education.

Like Collins, his counterpart who taught literacy, Escalante received criticism as well as praise. Prior to the insult by the Educational Testing Service, he was opposed by students, colleagues, and parents at Garfield even when attempting to implement his calculus program. According to the school's principal, Henry Gradillas, "Too many of our kids thought algebra was too hard for them. Too many parents agreed. Too many teachers and counselors accepted that the socioeconomic situation of these kids was so low that they could not handle higher math. It was attitudes, not socioeconomic status, that prevented these kids from succeeding."[14] Still, he persisted. As time went on, Escalante received numerous awards, including several honorary degrees and the Presidential Medal for Excellence in Education from Ronald Reagan.

Conclusion

All considered, what have we learned about challenging youth from these two extraordinary teachers? Collins and Escalante demonstrated that academic achievement has far more to do with the learner's personal attitude than with their level of innate intelligence. By now, you should have a firm grasp of what the Tubman Educator is, and why she/he is needed. It should also be clear that those who master measurement—be they Murray and Herrnstein, the Educational Testing Service, or the psychometricians in your local school system—are no match for those who master motivation, like Collins, Escalante . . . and you.

Challenge therefore deserves its place at the center of the FACES framework; for without it, our youth will never fulfill their God-given potential. Remember then this algorithm for challenging youth: Connection comes about as one cultivates positive and caring relationships; Direction provides not only rigorous training but also the guidance and instruction that enables youth to achieve consistently at high levels. I might add that the positive relationships and guidance that come from Connection and Direction could effectively counter the mental health concerns described in chapter 2. Following are seven fundamental steps that advocates should take to challenge youth effectively:

1. Reflect on the relationship between passion and rigor, discussed in this chapter.
2. Always communicate high expectations of youth.
3. Encourage youth to believe in themselves.
4. Insist that youth take personal responsibility.
5. Increase rather than reduce rigorous training.
6. Provide support to help youth reach higher levels of rigor.
7. Use "Connection" (relationship) to leverage the power of "Direction" (rigor and guidance).

Before ending this chapter, I believe it is both useful and important to consider the significance of these two outstanding educators. Although they worked with the nation's two largest ethnic minority groups (as of this writing), their accomplishments have much broader implications. Under the current paradigm in education, curriculum and instruction have been divided into three major categories: special education for students with disabilities, gifted and talented education, and regular education. Nationwide, considerable controversy surrounds these as well as other policies and practices that

Challenge: Using Connection and Direction

stem from that paradigm. In recent years, for instance, communities have been immersed in contentious debates about equity and fairness such as the gifted and talented education program in New York City Public Schools, the Supreme Court ruling on affirmative action in college admissions, and the alleged overidentification of children assigned to special education.

In light of the student achievement results observed in the work of Marva Collins and Jaime Escalante, why should we continue to cling to a paradigm whose basis has been proven false? The truth, for example, is not that most kids don't have the ability to excel in math. Rather, it is that math is often taught in ways that most kids apparently find difficult to learn. And how math is often taught reflects the educational paradigm that drives curriculum and instruction. To the same token, these two educators armed with a different paradigm enabled students to achieve consistently at high levels, despite having been from poverty-stricken communities and labeled as slow learners or even incapable of learning.

You might say that their accomplishment was tantamount to scoring a touchdown after starting from their own goal line. Now, if you're a recruiter looking for talented football players, how might you assess the performance of such kids, given their starting point? Can you see, therefore, why prioritizing test scores in deciding admissions at any level—whether preschool or college—is misguided? Tests miss the mark in predicting students' long-term performance because the latter has more to do with will than skill. Tests do not measure the former; they focus only on the latter. Thus, better ways of sorting kids into different educational programs are not what we need. Rather, what we need are better methods of helping all children to reach one common high standard of achievement. The only exception might be in cases of children with learning disorders that actually impede their ability to learn, as opposed to those who are designated as disabled, based on misguided assessments and labels.

Unfortunately, despite the exceptional demonstrations by Collins and Escalante decades ago, vast inequity in education persists. It might not surprise you to hear that course-taking requirements for high school graduation are, in general, set by state policymakers. But did you know that across the United States there are not one but *one hundred different high school graduation options*, and that among these *only seven states* require that graduation be based solely on the completion of a college- and career-ready (the most rigorous) course of study?[15] And, if I may push the envelope just a bit further: With an average of two graduation options for every state in the United States, how willing would you be to bet that the kids who graduate under the less rigorous options are more likely to resemble the kids taught by Collins and Escalante? Consider, as well, both the short- and long-term implications of a two-tiered educational system whenever you hear discussion of "rising" graduation rates. So, the same gap in expectations for student achievement that existed before you were even born persists relentlessly into the twenty-first century under the guise of legitimacy. Rise up, therefore, youth advocate! For it seems, as Malcolm X used to say, "You've been bamboozled!"[16]

Challenge: Using Connection and Direction

The new paradigm proposed in this book, however, advocates one high standard for all youth. Why?

By using a paradigm that emphasized personal effort rather than intellectual ability, both of our exemplars achieved extraordinary results with children and youth from the very bottom of America's socioeconomic ladder. Collins and Escalante strove to make their students willful, not just skillful. Both demonstrated that "ganas education" is more powerful than "gifted education." Essentially, both demonstrated that passion propels performance.

In closing, therefore, I challenge you again as I did in chapter 5 to embrace a paradigm that sees *all children* as gifted and to treat them accordingly. Perhaps the rationale for adopting this new paradigm is best understood through an anecdote told by Henry Gradillas, former principal at Garfield:

> We also had a lot of bright, hardworking kids who were never labeled gifted and talented (GT) because they lacked English skills in elementary school when monolingual English-speaking kids were being tested for GT. Others may not have had the IQ to qualify for GT, but they had the *ganas*, and they did well in higher-level classes . . . Escalante did not much like the GT label . . . Once, a student from a GT math class asked Escalante for help with a trigonometry problem. When the student explained that he was gifted, Escalante said, "This problem's for

boy scouts. I'm not going to waste my time explaining it. I'll let one of my students who's not gifted explain it to you."[17]

AUTHOR'S KEY POINTS

1. The FACES framework demands rigorous training to develop the potential in youth.
2. Use supportive relationships and guidance (Connection and Direction) to leverage rigor.
3. In general, advocates should apply one high standard of rigor to all youth.

Challenge: Using Connection and Direction

MY KEY REFLECTIONS

1. What in this chapter left the biggest impression on me?

2. What personal experiences, if any, did this chapter bring to mind?

3. What action might I or others take based on what I've learned?

CHAPTER 9

Expression: Cultivating Autonomy and Agency

Children enter school as question marks and leave as periods.

—Neil Postman, American educator and social critic

In the previous chapter, we learned not only how but why it is critical that youth be challenged in our educational programs. Doing so is indispensable preparation for the fourth feature of the FACES framework: EXPRESSION. Commonly referred to among educators as "voice and choice," this feature encourages young people not only to participate in the educational process but also—and much more importantly—to own it. Expression means that students should play an active role in their education, assuming greater responsibility for it as they grow.

Unfortunately, for many youngsters, the situation at school is precisely the opposite. In classrooms, learning is often passive rather than active. Further, students are treated as objects rather than subjects. The subjects of instruction at school typically include reading, mathematics, social studies, and science. Thus, some students may feel as if they are targets of instruction. As such, they have little or no say in what is to be learned or how. Worse still, they become a means to the educational system's end rather than vice versa. It should come as no surprise therefore that students often feel alienated from and apathetic about school.

Under the FACES framework, however, Expression is where the rubber meets the road. Here is where students take ownership of the learning process and begin to experience empowerment—the purpose of education. Since whatever they end up producing becomes an extension of themselves, Expression is ultimately where the value of education manifests itself. That value goes far beyond their GPA and SAT or ACT scores. Here is where the faces behind the numbers begin to shine. But for all this to happen, educators must make space for kids to express their own ideas and desires. Let's take a closer look, then, at what Expression means, its implications, and then . . . how it can be cultivated.

The Significance of Expression

Going back to the self-determination theory (SDT), discussed in chapters 2 and 5, let's trace our steps and connect the dots to understand the significance of Expression within the core of the FACES framework. First, in chapter 7, we discussed the meaning of Affirmation, which you may have noticed with its emphasis on validating youth, corresponds directly to the basic need for relatedness under SDT. Then, in chapter 8, we learned the importance of using positive relationships as the approach for challenging youth to be and do their best. As youth grow through rigorous training and challenge, they gradually fulfill the basic human need for competence in social affairs.

Here, in chapter 9, we touch upon the third basic psychological need encompassed by the theory: autonomy. In achieving competence, youth become skillful—but not necessarily willful. The latter trait is an essential feature of the new educational paradigm proposed in this book: Passion propels performance. Thus, the significance of Expression now comes to light: Through autonomy, youth learn to make choices and decisions to determine their own destinies. In short, autonomy leads to agency.

Expression starts with teachers encouraging students to voice their preferences in the early years of schooling and ends with students driving the educational process increasingly as they progress through the pipeline. As a result, by the time they reach high school, students should be nothing less than powerful; competent and confident; aware of their strengths and weaknesses, their likes and dislikes. Moreover, equipped with this awareness, they become spiritually and emotionally ready to make their unique contributions to the world.

Can you imagine the impression such a young person might make on a college admissions officer or a prospective employer? Why, they'd be blown away for sure! Unfortunately, so many of our youth pale in comparison to their potential, and not because they are incapable but because their potential was barely nurtured. And it was not nurtured because that was never the end goal in the first place. Again, the aim of conventional schooling is to make youth skillful not willful. One can become skillful by developing a capable yet compliant mind. To become willful, however, requires growth mentally, emotionally, and spiritually. Putting it yet another way, educator and social critic Neil Postman has rightly said that children enter school as question marks and leave as periods.[1] Through Expression and the FACES framework, however, youth clearly will not leave school as periods, but instead—as exclamation points!

How to Cultivate Expression in Youth

With an understanding of what Expression means, let's move forward by examining some examples of how to cultivate this feature in young people. The first of two examples I have chosen for this task is a community-based organization located in the nation's capital. The second is a nonprofit organization that operates in New York City. It has been an honor to collaborate with both, incidentally as previous clients.

Expression: Cultivating Autonomy and Agency

United to Rise (U2R), formerly Youth Organizations United to Rise (YOUR), has provided enrichment learning activities to more than five thousand youth in Washington, DC, since its inception.[2] Like many community-based organizations in urban areas, U2R primarily serves kids from pre-kindergarten through high school presumed to be at risk of academic failure. On account of its success with such youth, three of DC's recent mayors, local government agencies, and the *Washington Post* and *Times* have recognized U2R for the effectiveness of its out-of-school-time programming. According to its current executive director, Talib Madyun, 85 percent of former student participants have graduated from high school, and 77 percent have attended college.

All this began with Mrs. Joyce Madyun, an educator who worked for the District of Columbia Public Schools. In the fall of 1988, she opened her home to children attending West Elementary School nearby, noticing their need for a safe place before and after school. Almost ten years later, she and her husband purchased a dilapidated house, which they refurbished and converted into an out-of-school-time center for the community in 1997.

Today, as of this writing, her son, Talib, heads the organization and shared information with me about how U2R has achieved its results.[3] To begin, the program's curriculum includes a heavy dose of mentoring, which builds supportive relationships with students. It also offers an array of social-emotional learning activities, games, and enrichment opportunities that keep students interested and engaged so they learn more.

One of the main ingredients I observed is the program's emphasis on empowering students through self-expression. Active rather than passive participation appears to be the rule at U2R. I found some examples of how students demonstrate self-expression on a YouTube video in response to the question, "What do you like about YOUR community center?" Here's a brief sample of their heartfelt replies:[4]

Yvette, fourth grader: "I like to do art, drawing, and math."

Jeremy, second grader: "You can focus on your homework."

Lisa, first grader: "My favorite activity here at YOUR is to play board games and color."

Steven, sixth grader: "I get to go on a computer and work with technology."

The video also shows students directing themselves in caroling, though off-key at times, the venerable anthem: "Lift Every Voice and Sing."

As a viewer, you may notice that the students speak incorrectly at times in terms of grammar and usage. The point here, however, is that the value of self-expression, particularly at their level, lies not in the precision of the expression but in the opportunity to have it at all. Allowing students autonomy to express themselves sends the message that their opinions matter—and thus they themselves are valued. Moreover, as students progress through the program at higher grade levels, their ability to express themselves naturally improves. Increasingly, the program solicits students' input into designing activities as well as in surveys used to evaluate activities. U2R also cultivates self-expression among teens through its signature leadership

Expression: Cultivating Autonomy and Agency

programs, Renaissance Man (for boys) and Petals of Primrose (for girls). Over time, all of these activities help youth to develop self-direction, confidence, and a sense of control over their lives. In other words, they become willful as well as skillful.

One of the most impressive organizations cultivating the ability of youth to express themselves today has been around for quite some time. Since 1980, Youth Communication (YC) has been giving voice to high school students in New York City. According to Executive Director Betsy Cohen: "Youth Communication's vision is to create a more empathic world for and with our young people so they feel represented, heard, and supported to achieve their dreams."[5] Notice the connections here to autonomy and agency. The world that YC envisions calls for youth to participate in its creation as well as assume personal responsibility for making their own a reality.

YC's mission is to create more supportive learning communities in order to elevate youth voices through personal stories. The mission is implemented through a curriculum based on the principles of social-emotional learning (SEL). Toward this end, in recent years, its curriculum has been implemented by more than fifty schools and agencies, including New York City Public Schools, Mastery Charter Network (in Philadelphia), Horizons National, and the Girl Scouts of Greater New York. In the last five years, the organization has trained more than five thousand educators, impacting more than one hundred thousand youth across the nation.

Consistent with the new paradigm proposed in this book, YC places a great deal of emphasis on cultivating a supportive learning environment as a strategy to improve student achievement. YC uses personal stories developed in a rigorous writing program to show teens how to make positive changes in their lives. As you might imagine, the organization and its students have been the recipients of many and diverse awards. After all, despite one's age, don't we all like a good story?

Consider this testimonial from Principal Lori Krane, for instance: "YC's stories and lessons really get my kids' wheels turning. I GET CHILLS listening to them ask questions and talk to each other."[6]

The stories these young authors tell are often provocative. I imagine this contributes to the cathartic effects that the youth might experience by writing them. I'm going to share an extensive excerpt from a story I recently read through YC's publication, *Represent*, featured as Story of the Week:[7]

> When I was 7, a family member began sexually abusing me, and my parents found out four years later, when I was 11. My mom blamed me, but I hadn't expected her to understand or sympathize with me. She'd been cold and critical of me my whole life. I did, however, expect my dad to protect me and tell me it was not my fault. Instead, he looked at me with disgust, as if I had asked for this to happen to me. That hurt more than my mother's blame.
>
> . . . I became distant and withdrawn. Being around my family hurt in ways I couldn't explain.

I couldn't understand how my own father could hurt me so much. I became rude and challenged them; the sweet, quiet daughter was not there anymore. I locked myself in my room and took sleeping pills I stole from my mother. When I was sleeping, they couldn't bother me and I didn't have to feel my pain.

My dad was the first man in my life to break my heart and my trust, by making me feel like it was my fault that I was being sexually abused. Even my rapist did not hurt me as much as my dad did. He made me feel worthless by ignoring me for months after this horrible thing I experienced and not even stopping it . . .

I am 20 now, and for the last four years in foster care I have been avoiding my parents. Being around my parents made me feel like someone was stabbing my heart over and over again.

I have blocked their number, and even though they have tried to reestablish a relationship with me, I want nothing to do with them. I do not want to know anything about them, and I do not want them to know anything about me. To me, both my parents are dead, and I am an orphan. (I have an OK but distant relationship with my siblings.) People in my life know that something bad happened in my family, and foster care workers know the details. I prefer not to talk about it in general. I have done therapy for two years and I have learned enough skills there to navigate my emotions, for now.

A complete separation from my parents helps me move forward from the pain of their betrayal. As does keeping myself very busy. I did become my role model in the end. I finished my BA in two years with a 3.9 GPA and will soon start graduate school.

It's obvious why the young woman who wrote this story preferred to remain anonymous. I hope as well that, after reading it, you can appreciate more fully the value of the work YC and organizations like it are doing. Telling one's own story is an exercise in autonomy that promotes agency. By authoring their own stories, youth learn that they can also write the script of their own lives. They can determine, therefore, whether they will be portrayed as victims of circumstances or victors over them.

Conclusion

You, then, the youth advocate, must promote Expression by enabling students to adapt school to their needs rather than adapt to the needs of school. To cultivate autonomy and agency in youth, enable the following into educational activities:

Expression: Cultivating Autonomy and Agency

1. Allow youth to contribute to your school or educational program increasingly as they age. Three practical ways of accomplishing this are:
   a. Survey students to determine their interests for incorporation into the curriculum;
   b. Survey students to get their feedback on the existing activities in order to make appropriate modifications (for an excellent example, revisit "The DAP Effect" in chapter 6);[8] and
   c. Implement traditional opportunities such as student-led presentations, student committees, and board representatives.
2. Allow youth opportunities to choose and engage in activities that interest them personally. Ideally (like YC), provide structured support for them in those activities.
3. Finally (like U2R), provide opportunities for personal and social growth through customized youth leadership development programs.

Ultimately, you want to make your students feel that they are partners, rather than objects, in the educational process. As a result of Expression, apathy and alienation will cease to exist in our schools. Ownership and responsibility will replace passivity and disengagement. As the walls of compliance and conformity that uphold schooling give way to autonomy and agency, school will take on a new meaning. It will become the place where dreams are discovered, inspired, and nurtured rather than where, as Tony Wagner suggested in chapter 1, they remain dormant, discouraged, or ignored. Then, we will finally come to know school as the place made for our children rather than the reverse.[9]

Having effectively explored Fun, Affirmation, Challenge, and Expression, the stage of youth empowerment is now set for the last and all-important feature of the FACES framework: Success.

AUTHOR'S KEY POINTS

1. Expression, the fourth feature of the FACES framework, requires the development of agency and autonomy in youth.

2. Expression is the feature where students begin to experience competence, control, and thus empowerment, which is the overall purpose of education.

3. Through Expression, therefore, the FACES framework enables youth to become skillful as well as willful through education.

MY KEY REFLECTIONS

1. What in this chapter left the biggest impression on me?

2. What personal experiences, if any, did this chapter bring to mind?

3. What action might I or others take based on what I've learned?

CHAPTER 10

Success: Principles for Prosperity

If you plan on being anything less than what you are capable of being, you will probably be unhappy all the days of your life.

—Abraham Maslow, American psychologist and philosopher

Alas, we have arrived at the fifth and final feature of the FACES framework: Success. This chapter discusses that all-important yet elusive goal virtually everyone seeks. If you've observed carefully, you'll see how the four previous features prepare one for achieving it.

The first feature, Fun, primes youth by putting them in a positive emotional state, one conducive to learning. Effective teachers and mentors then use this state to promote emotional fulfillment for optimal youth development. Doing so involves the three core features of the FACES framework as discussed in the previous chapter (Affirmation, Challenge, and Expression). These equip youth with the self-confidence, the skills, and the sense of agency needed to begin charting their own destiny. Combined, the four features lead one to empowerment, which is the overarching purpose of education that we identified in chapter 5.

Now you are ready to place the cherry on the top of the cake. To do so, it is necessary to revisit the second of the big three questions that we examined back in chapter 5. Specifically, we need to return to the question: What is the purpose of education? In that chapter, I declared unequivocally that the purpose of education is empowerment. Education should enhance one's ability to be effective in life beyond school, to exercise greater control and influence over one's affairs. Consequently, education should help to elevate one's quality of life.

In this chapter, I offer a specific strategy for achieving this ultimate purpose. In my humble opinion, one has the best chance of becoming successful by becoming empowered. And one becomes most empowered when one achieves the level of personal development that the renowned American psychologist Abraham Maslow called self-actualization.[1]

Self-actualization is where we begin to fulfill our purpose and potential. This stage of personal development often takes one beyond the realm of competence to a place where creativity reigns supreme. The stage stems from the congruence between one's potential and its gratification. Self-actualization is not, therefore, merely a matter of achievement. Rather, it exists when one experiences emotional fulfillment through the meaningfulness of achievement.

Self-actualization is often equated with the "flow state" popularized by another well-known psychologist, Mihaly Csikszentmihalyi.[2] But whereas flow describes a state or feeling in the moment resulting from a specific activity, self-actualization is better understood, for our purposes, as the result of a particular role that facilitates peak emotional experiences over time. In other words, to achieve self-actualization, one must occupy a role or a vocation where one's interests and talents can be expressed and fulfilled repeatedly. Oprah Winfrey suggests the same in asserting: "Follow your passion. It will lead you to your purpose."[3]

Importantly, herein lies a critical missing link between conventional education and the real world for which it ostensibly prepares youth. Because of school's tendency to suppress rather than nurture passion, many students never seek self-actualization but only a "good-paying job" instead. This is precisely what happened in chapter 3 to Robert Harris, the young man who unfortunately realized the folly of this approach only after dropping out of the university, saddled in debt. His experience remains a classic example of school getting in the way of the education one needs to truly succeed.

Under the FACES framework, the advocate must intentionally teach success, just like any other subject. It is not to be left to chance. In doing so, self-knowledge is the key, for it determines how one uses their knowledge and skills to contribute to others and thereby secure one's own livelihood. Self-knowledge therefore is the starting point—not the technical knowledge and skills that we acquire in school. Self-knowledge is the light that shows each one of us our unique way toward self-actualization. In teaching success, the advocate's end goal is to help their young people figure out the role or vocation wherein to place themselves to achieve self-actualization.

How to Teach Youth to Succeed

Self-actualization, however, is about achieving success in the long run. It is equally important, if not more so, that youth experience success in the short run. Doing so is consistent with the development of competence, discussed previously as one of three theoretical pillars of the FACES framework. Experiencing success in the present also closes the cycle of the framework because achievement fulfills one emotionally. Success feels good. And that pleasure inspires one to engage all over again in the learning process. The best way for youth to learn about success, therefore, is for them to experience it in their current reality, not in the distant future as though it were part of planning for retirement.

To help youth learn how to become successful in both the short and long term, the FACES framework requires that advocates intentionally teach them success principles. Young people should not have to reinvent the wheel of achievement when such information is abundantly available. That being said, now I'm going to give you my special recipe for accomplishing this task. Ladies and gentlemen, I'm going to share what I call "The Seven Prosperity Principles for Youth Success":

1. Passion
2. Purpose
3. People
4. Perspective
5. Preparation
6. Performance
7. Persistence

Given the diversity of educational programs, I would not pretend to provide a one-size-fits-all approach to implementing the principles. That, in my humble opinion, must be tailored to your particular organization and setting. Implementing them in middle school, for example, would look quite different from doing so at the university level. Notwithstanding the need for customization, you can and should make these principles an integral part of your educational program, whether in regular school, after school, or home school, whether at a college or a university. The meaning and value of these seven principles, as follows, are presented with older youth in mind.

Principle #1: Passion

Desire is the starting point of all achievement.[4]

—**Napoleon Hill, author, *Think and Grow Rich***

Passion, we have learned, is the seed of enthusiasm within each of us that must be nurtured to flourish. Your first and foremost job as a youth advocate is to aid young people in finding theirs. Whatever the nature of your educational program, therefore, provide youth with ample opportunities to explore diverse interests to learn what specifically they enjoy doing. Students' passions may be multiple and may change over time. The important thing is that they become and remain aware of their passions, which is the first step toward achieving self-actualization.

Principle #2: Purpose

Knowing yourself and what you want you to do is one of the most important things you'll ever do in this life.[5]

—**John C. Maxwell, leadership expert and author**

Purpose gives both meaning and direction to one's life. Your job as an advocate is to help youth figure out how to translate their passion into a definite role and arena. As youth grow, encourage them to think about how they might like to contribute to society as an adult. At every stage in their development, you want to help them to identify not merely the things they enjoy but also how they might use their interests and talents to serve others. Encourage them to think big, without limitations as to what they might do or become. At the same time, respect that ultimately the decision is theirs. Whether they decide that self-actualization means becoming an effective parent or a U.S. president is up to them.

Principle #3: People

Seek out positive people who have achieved the success you want to create in your own life.[6]

—**Darren Hardy, personal development expert and author**

The role that people play in one's success (or lack thereof) cannot be overstated. Our relationships with others are extremely powerful because they influence how we see ourselves and the world. Our beliefs, habits, and behaviors are all affected by the people with whom we regularly associate. You, the advocate, therefore, must impress upon youth that they should carefully develop personal and professional relationships with three time-tested keys in mind. One, for better or worse, we become like the company we keep, hence the old saying: "Birds of a feather flock together." Two, another familiar saying: "It's not what you know but who you know," is also true. Knowing the "right" people can make the doors of opportunity much easier to open. And three, perhaps more than anything else in life, the quality of our relationships affects our overall well-being. Whether the circumstances be personal or professional, one of the greatest resources that anyone can have is helpful people.

Principle #4: Perspective

The way we see governs how we behave.[7]

—Stephen R. Covey, author,
The 7 Habits of Highly Effective People

I have placed this principle in the center of the list for a special reason. Perspective gets to the heart of the matter regarding this book, which advocates shifting the education paradigm. Perspective deals with how we see the world and, most importantly, ourselves. The critical role of perspective in shaping the quality of one's life is embodied in the assertion by renowned success coach Anthony Robbins that "Success is 80% psychology and only 20% skill."[8] If Robbins is right, then the process of education (schooling) must never be allowed to obstruct or erode the purpose of education (empowerment).

The FACES framework therefore charges the youth advocate with the sacred responsibility of cultivating in youth a perspective that honors their divinity as creatures made in the image of the Divine. Such a perspective demands that they see themselves as the authors and architects of their lives. Accordingly, they must assume personal responsibility, believing that they have the power to make a difference in their affairs. Moreover, as discussed in chapter 5, encourage youth to see the world as it is, rather than as a reflection of themselves; for without an accurate map of reality, true prosperity cannot be attained.

Principle #5: Preparation

If you don't design your own life, chances are you'll fall into someone else's plan. And guess what they have planned for you? Not much.[9]

—Jim Rohn

Youth advocates must teach youth how to make practical plans for success. The seven principles for prosperity presented in this chapter constitute a general plan or framework for such. Still, a more detailed and personal form of planning needs to be done for each person. Such a plan provides clear and specific action steps to increase the probability of achieving one's desired outcome.

With undergraduate students, I recommend including career exploration as regular counseling each semester if not as a standalone course. By aligning one's studies with one's interests and skills, students are far more likely to persist in college and secure a meaningful job by the time they leave. At Harvard, for example, expository writing is a required course for all first-year students to develop their writing skills. Students meet regularly in small groups and receive one-on-one feedback from instructors. Why not do the same with career planning each semester instead of starting in the senior year, as is usually the case? The improper attention to career preparation is indeed the Achilles heel of higher education. The same fosters unemployment, underemployment, and college loan debt (see chapter 3).

Principle #6: Performance

The secret to getting results that last is to never stop making improvements.[10]

—James Clear, *Atomic Habits*

Commencement exercises at the university are named such because they signify the beginning of one's journey of performance, having completed a major milestone in preparation. But, as John Maxwell pointed out in one of his outstanding books, *The 15 Invaluable Laws of Growth*, if you are going to fulfill your potential and increase your value to others, then you must constantly engage in a personal process of continuous improvement. This is what Stephen Covey called "sharpening the saw," and why Jim Rohn urged his protégés to "work harder on yourself than you do on your job."[11] Therefore, youth advocates must instill in their protégés the understanding that success depends on a commitment to constantly increasing their knowledge and skills. Formal education is not the finish line but merely a point of departure.

Principle #7: Persistence

Paralyze resistance with persistence.[12]

—Woody Hayes, American football player and coach

Despite all other principles and virtues, those intent on achieving anything must be ready to embrace persistence. After all, how realistic is it to expect that anything will go just as planned the first time? Not very. Consistently, life experience teaches the value of patience by delaying the fulfillment of our desires, often rewarding only those who persist toward their goals. Ironically, the advocate must instill the indispensable principle of persistence in youth by teaching them the ironic relationship between success and failure. For as John Maxwell asserts: "When it comes right down to it, I know of only one factor that separates those who consistently shine from those who don't: *The difference between average people and achieving people is their perception of and response to failure.*"[13]

The power of persistence is beautifully illustrated by Darren Hardy in his bestseller *The Compound Effect*. Early in the book, Hardy explains how small actions executed consistently over time either make us or break us.[14] He demonstrates that if you had a single penny that doubled in value every day, in less than one month you'd be a millionaire. Did you get that? (Doing the same demonstration, by the way, would be an excellent activity to implement with your students. Try it!) In his concise manual on success, Hardy teaches that outstanding achievement typically is a process of executing the right habits and activities over time as opposed to the occurrence of a single major event. In other words, success is a process, a journey rather than a destination.

Speaking of which, we now have reached the end of our journey together, not only through the seven prosperity principles, but also the five features of the FACES framework. It now should be clear that FACES enables youth to see and feel themselves at the center of education, and also why this matters (see Figure 8). By adding Success to the previous four features, FACES prepares youth for the journey of self-actualization. Most importantly, we have learned that the starting point for achieving this end is self-knowledge. Self-knowledge is the lens through which students must interpret their education; for only then can they become willful as well as skillful. This chapter, therefore, has provided them with both a compass and a map to navigate the sea of life, not merely as sailors aboard vessels adrift, but as captains commanding their ships in pursuit of destinies only they can determine.

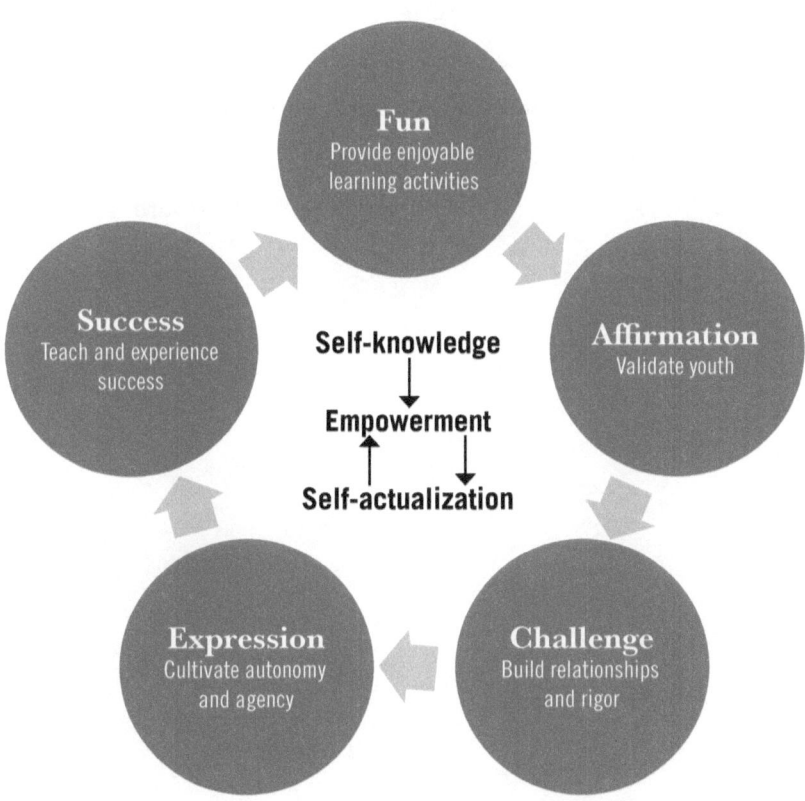

Figure 8. The Faces Framework for a New Paradigm in Education: Passion Propels Performance!

AUTHOR'S KEY POINTS

1. Under the FACES framework, advocates must teach youth explicitly about success.

2. The seven prosperity principles discussed herein provide a map, while self-actualization serves as the practical goal and compass for achieving success.

3. Self-knowledge is the starting point in the journey of success.

MY KEY REFLECTIONS

1. What in this chapter left the biggest impression on me?

2. What personal experiences, if any, did this chapter bring to mind?

3. What action might I or others take based on what I've learned?

Conclusion

Dear youth advocate, what a pleasure it has been for me to share this journey with you! In closing, let's review where we have been and what we have learned along the way.

We began by identifying the subtle yet serious problem that afflicts young people, regardless of their socioeconomic status: alienation from school. Through students' own voices, we learned how schooling, the formal process of instruction, can interfere with education, the desired outcome of instruction. Far too many youth find school to be an alienating experience. As a result, underachievement and disengagement from school are commonplace. Alienation from school is a problem that afflicts the nation's youth in general. It is not confined, as some choose to believe, to those outside the social mainstream. To bring this point home, we saw how alienation from school—and its consequences—acts like a virus that moves with its victims from school to the workplace to society in issues that may ultimately impact everyday life. Moreover, the greatest potential threat of alienation from school is alienation from self, for self-knowledge is the foundation for success.

We also learned that alienation from school may vary from one educational institution to another. Undoubtedly, there are schools across the nation that offer wonderful educational opportunities for youth, as we reviewed some excellent examples. Unfortunately, however, the overarching paradigm that guides the thinking of many educators undermines the chances that youth will experience such opportunities. As evidence, we learned that even in schools renowned for academic excellence, underachievement and disengagement can easily be observed at alarming levels. Consequently, this book advocates for a new paradigm that addresses the root of the problem in education. In short, how we see education *is* the problem.

To illustrate this point, we contrasted two metaphors: the Broccoli Model of Education, representing the current system, and the Pumpkin Muffin Model to convey the new educational paradigm and process. The former model emphasizes innate ability and rigorous coursework as keys to prepare one with knowledge and skills for higher education or the workforce. In contrast, the latter model focuses on one's spiritual and emotional development as fundamental for success in school and beyond. In contrasting these perspectives, we went back to square one and examined three fundamental questions about education:

1. What is education?
2. What is the purpose of education?

3. What should the educational process look like to achieve that purpose?

After exploring these questions, the remainder of the book provided the FACES framework as a practical strategy for bringing the Pumpkin Muffin Model to fruition. The framework, displayed as a flowchart on the last page of this conclusion, consists of five components or features:

- Fun
- Affirmation
- Challenge
- Expression
- Success

These are the practical steps that youth advocates, especially those whom I referred to as Tubman Educators, can take to truly empower youth to lead happy and prosperous lives. And in doing so, you will transform not only education, but also society, elevating it to a higher level in general by doing the same for every individual youth.

Although we learned about two quintessential Tubman Educators, this work would be remiss if it did not underscore the importance of the educational administrator. Amid poor working conditions, which included little administrative support, Marva Collins left her teacher job to establish her own school. And let's not forget the experience that teacher

Don't Let School Get in the Way of Education

Sarah Fine had with her administrator (see chapter 6), which encouraged her to leave the profession. Jaime Escalante, on the other hand, received strong support from his principal, which enhanced his success as a teacher. The leadership of principals and superintendents will always be a key factor in schools because leadership either stymies or supports the work of teachers. As orchestrators of school culture and climate, the educational administrator either magnifies or diminishes the effectiveness of teachers, which research suggests is one of the most influential factors in student achievement, if not the most influential.[1]

Alas, allow me to highlight one particularly noteworthy study that I believe signals the potential value of the FACES framework in education. Funded in part by the Gates Foundation with a budget of $237 million, this study on teacher effectiveness spanned six years and involved seven sites across the United States. The primary aim of the initiative was to increase student achievement among low-income minority students by increasing their access to effective teachers. The project was as sophisticated as it was extensive, having been designed by those who might rightly be called the Masters of Measurement. Yet, after all was said and done, the project had no effect on student achievement. The initiative did succeed, however, in measuring what researchers believed were the key characteristics of effective teaching that would leverage achievement. Among several explanations for the lack of impact on students, the study included the following:

Conclusion

A near-exclusive focus on teacher effectiveness might be insufficient to dramatically improve student outcomes. Many other factors might need to be addressed, ranging from early childhood education, to students' social and emotional competencies, to the school learning environment, to family support.[2]

Thus, the study's results bring to mind a most befitting observation embraced by Albert Einstein: "Not everything that can be measured counts; and not everything that counts can be measured."[3]

That being said, ever so eloquently I assert, at the risk of sounding pretentious, that had those schools implemented the ideas contained in this book, they certainly would have achieved much better results. The same can be said for Bill and Melinda Gates had they hired me as their education consultant, and I would have given them a much better price!

In closing, I'd like to underscore the need for FACES by sharing a personal story that took place more than twenty years after I began my career in education as a young substitute teacher in the public schools of New York City.

My wife, Andrea, and I were filled with excitement as we cruised down the highway to spend the Thanksgiving Day holiday with friends. The ride from our home was absolutely delightful. Beautiful shades of yellow, orange, red, and brown adorned the trees all along the way, accentuating the cozy feeling that epitomizes the fall season. Arthur and Elaine were kind and generous people whom we had met only recently through Andrea, who had roomed with Elaine during the summer while working on her master's degree in teaching. I, meanwhile, was employed full time in Fairfax County Public Schools as an evaluator of educational programs, advising the superintendent's leadership team. Highly regarded for excellence in academic achievement, the district operated more than two hundred schools with as many superintendents as some schools have teachers. To this day, I recall the two years spent in "FCPS" as one of the best professional experiences of my career.

Upon our arrival, we quickly unloaded our bags and then accepted Arthur's invitation to enjoy a coffee break before heading out for some provisions. While Arthur prepared coffee in the kitchen, Elaine introduced us to the two young people seated in the main room in front of the television. "Kids, I'd like you to meet Andrea and Anane, the friends that I told you will spend Thanksgiving with us." Turning toward us, she continued, "Guys, this is Kevin, my son, and Brittany, my niece." We cheerfully exchanged handshakes. Both seemed to be typical teens, with Brittany clearly more chipper than her cousin.

As we finished some delicious pumpkin spiced coffee, Elaine asked if we would accompany them in their van to do some last-minute shopping for the festivities ahead. "Sure," replied Andrea.

Conclusion

"Kids, you're welcome to join us," said Arthur.

"Actually, I wouldn't mind the ride," replied Brittany. Kevin meanwhile didn't react one way or another.

"Okay, son, we'll be back soon enough," said Elaine. And we headed out.

Knowing that the trip to the shopping center would take about twenty minutes, Elaine began filling us in almost immediately on the family situation. "So, Andrea, it wouldn't surprise me if you and Anane have already detected that Kevin can be a little reserved."

"Oh, really?" I interrupted. "That's fine. I myself have that tendency," I added with a slight chuckle.

"Well, I think I'd feel better if you knew what's going on behind the scenes in our house. It also might make your stay a little easier," replied Elaine.

The story that Elaine told us was somber. She and Arthur had adopted Kevin about ten years earlier while doing missionary work through their church in Latin America, where he was without a family and destitute. They sought to give him a better life by bringing him to the United States. This didn't mean that their home was perfect. Of course, like any other, it had its own challenges. Nonetheless, they loved Kevin all they could, but the situation never fully clicked. Unfortunately, school never helped much, as the boy encountered few peers and teachers with whom he could relate personally. Now at age sixteen, he was at risk of dropping out.

We arrived at the shopping center just in time to break the air of despair that seemed to be filling the van. Thank God!

However, the conversation on our way back home was almost as disturbing.

I thought I would strike up a conversation of a different tone by asking Brittany how high school was going. Without hesitation, she affirmed: "I'm doing pretty good as far as grades are concerned, but I don't feel like I'm learning a lot."

"What do you mean?" I asked.

"Well, we spend a lot of time testing. So, what I do is study for that, but afterward I don't feel like I've really learned anything."

"And what are your grades like, if you don't mind my asking?"

"Oh, I'm doing great. I have an A average," she replied.

Given the irony of the situation, I couldn't hold back on telling everyone about how deeply concerning I thought both cases were. On the one hand, Elaine and Arthur's immigrant son from Latin America was performing poorly in school, while on the other hand, their niece—seemingly the epitome of the successful American high school student—was ostensibly succeeding. In reality, both were undoubtedly suffering from the subtle and insidious problem of alienation from school.

Our conversation did end on a good note, however, as we arrived home and backed the van into the driveway. I shared my vision of creating an organization that would close the gap between education and emotional fulfillment for youth. "Whatever the specific form of organization," I explained, "the outcome would be the same: to make schooling an engaging and affirming experience."

Conclusion

"Wow!" replied Elaine. "Imagine that: school . . . an engaging and affirming experience."

Since that time, through my work as an education consultant, I have made presentations to audiences nationwide as well as abroad, sharing the FACES framework. The experiences of youth like Kevin and Brittany, Jeff Bliss, and Edmund Perry have inspired me to write this book. It is my hope that youth advocates, wherever found, will use FACES to bring about a transformation in education that will help liberate the gift awaiting cultivation in every child.

Support the Mission

With the welfare of all youth in mind, this book has been written as a source of knowledge and inspiration to be laid upon the edifice of truth, the construction of which is never ending. If you would like to support this mission, your contribution would be welcomed and appreciated. To that end, I humbly ask for your assistance by committing yourself to completing any three of the following **right now** (today's date:_____).

1. If you enjoyed the book, kindly leave a review at your favorite store: _____
   _____

2. Share this book with one or more persons:
   a. Name _____
   b. Name _____
   c. Name _____

3. Join my mailing list to receive news and resources related to this mission at: https://www.DrOinspires.com.

4. Help the book to reach a wider audience by sharing on social media using the hashtag #DrOinspires:
   a. _____
   b. _____
   c. _____

Thank you, and God bless.

Acknowledgments

I am grateful to the universe for the inspiration to fulfill this work, despite all adversity. I especially wish to thank my wife, Andrea, for encouraging me to tell my story and for her tremendous support of my journey as an author. I also thank Rukshani Lye-Ugwattage, my research assistant, who contributed immensely to writing this book.

I wish to extend gratitude to the following individuals who, in various ways, supported this work: Eric Brown, John T. Curtis, Annie J. Daniel, Nancy Day, Raquel Figueroa, Monty Fontenot, Sean J. Goodwin, Chad Green, Julissa Gutierrez-Hernández, Peter Kernion, Joshua Masterson, Father Louis Molinelli, Matthew R. Neely, McKinley Tim Rogers III, Denis Rousselle, Kenneth St. Charles, John C. Stewart, Casey Taylor, Jack Truxillo, Jenni Vega, and Ronda Williams.

Notes

Introduction

1. Ethan Yazzie-Mintz and Kim McCormick, "Finding the Humanity in the Data: Understanding, Measuring, and Strengthening Student Engagement," in *Handbook of Research on Student Engagement* (New York: Springer, 2012), 752.

2. Zach Hrynowski, "K-12 Schools Struggle to Engage Gen Z Students," Gallup.com, August 21, 2024, https://news.gallup.com/poll/648896/schools-struggle-engage-gen-students.aspx.

3. Grant Stringer, "Nais Report on the 2022 High School Survey of Student Engagement (HSSSE)," NAIS, accessed September 10, 2024, https://www.nais.org/articles/pages/research/nais-research-report-on-the-2022-high-school-survey-of-student-engagement-hssse/.

4. Russell W. Rumberger and Sun Ah Lim, *Why Students Drop Out of School: A Review of 25 Years of Research*, California Dropout Research Project Report #15 (Santa Barbara, CA: University of California, October 2008), https://www.issuelab.org/resources/11658/11658.pdf.

5. Joel McFarland, *Trends in High School Dropout and Completion Rates in the United States: 2019* (Washington, DC: U.S. Department of Education, January 2020), https://nces.ed.gov/pubs2020/2020117.pdf; Melanie Hanson, "College Dropout Rates," Education Data Initiative, updated August 16, 2024, https://educationdata.org/college-dropout-rates.

6. Hanson, "College Dropout Rates."

7. "What Can Students Do to Improve Their Chances of Finding Employment after College?," Disabilities, Opportunities, Internetworking, and Technology, University of Washington, updated April 9, 2021, https://www.washington.edu/doit/what-can-students-do-improve-their-chances-finding-employment-after-college.

8. E. Paul Zehr, "Mind Over Brain: Your Will Must Be Stronger Than Your Skill," *Psychology Today*, February 19, 2016, https://www.psychologytoday.com/us/blog/black-belt-brain/201602/mind-over-brain-your-will-must-be-stronger-your-skill.

9. *Oxford English Dictionary*, s.v. "lawdy," accessed September 10, 2024, https://www.oed.com/search/dictionary/?scope=Entries&q=lawdy. According to the *OED*, the word "lawdy" is a variant of "lordy," an expression of surprise and amazement. Here a play on words is used with the Latin *laude* (meaning "praise") and "lawdy," which are pronounced similarly. Thus, in contrast to the conventional graduation titles of academic distinction known as cum laude, magna cum laude, and summa cum laude, "Thank ya, Lawdy" jokingly suggests that the title bearer has graduated only by the grace of God.

Chapter 1

1. Over the course of my own career, I have worked with several of these policies and initiatives, including: The Elementary and Secondary Education Act (1965); The Education for All

Handicapped Children Act (1975); National Educational Goals (Educate America Act, 1994); No Child Left Behind Act (2001); The Common Core State Standards Initiative (2009); The Every Student Succeeds Act (2015); funding for the socioeconomically disadvantaged; Smaller Learning Communities Program; Professional Learning Communities; and Charter Schools.

2. Veronique Irwin, Ke Wang, Julie Jung, Erika Kessler, Tabitha Tezil, Sara Alhassani, Alison Filbey, et al., *Report on the Condition of Education 2024* (Washington, DC: National Department of Education, May 2024), 23, https://nces.ed.gov/pubs2024/2024144.pdf.

3. "Results from the 2019 Mathematics and Reading Assessments at Grade 12," The Nation's Report Card, accessed October 7, 2024, https://www.nationsreportcard.gov/mathematics/supportive_files/2019_infographic_G12_math_reading.pdf.

4. Dr. Anane Olatunji, Facing the Broccoli Model of Education, video, n.d., https://www.droinspires.com/book-dr-olatunji-landing-pg.

5. Ethan Yazzie-Mintz, *Charting the Path from Engagement to Achievement: A Report on the 2009 High School Survey of Student Engagement* (Bloomington, IN: Center for Evaluation and Education Policy, 2009), 6, https://web.archive.org/web/20100618132118/http://ceep.indiana.edu/hssse/images/HSSSE_2010_Report.pdf.

6. *2016 Gallup® Student Poll: A Snapshot of Results and Findings* (Washington, DC: Gallup, September 2016).

7. Steven J. Ingels, Daniel J. Pratt, Deborah R. Herget, Laura J. Burns, Jill A. Dever, Randolph Ottem, James E. Rogers, Ying Jin, Steve Leinwand, and Laura LoGerfo, *High School Longitudinal Study of 2009* (Washington, DC: U.S. Department of Education, July 2011), https://nces.ed.gov/surveys/hsls09/pdf/2011328_1.pdf.

8. "Effects of Bullying," stopbullying.gov, accessed November 22, 2024.

Don't Let School Get in the Way of Education

9. "Student's Classroom Rant Goes Viral," CNN.com, May 10, 2013, https://www.cnn.com/videos/us/2013/05/10/pkg-viral-student-rant.wfaa.

10. "Suli Breaks—Why I Hate School But Love Education [Official Spoken Word Video]," YouTube, 6:07, December 2, 2012, https://www.youtube.com/watch?v=y_ZmM7zPLyI.

11. Ram Castillo, "Prince Ea on Reaching Over 1 Billion Video Views and 10 Million Subscribers by Spreading Positive Social Change," *Giant Thinkers Podcast*, December 19, 2017, https://podcasts.apple.com/us/podcast/prince-ea-on-reaching-over-1-billion-video-views-and/id1001095170?i=1000397738897.

12. Richard Williams [Prince Ea], "I Sued the School System," YouTube, accessed October 7, 2024, directed by Bergvall and Lombardi, https://www.youtube.com/watch?v=dqTTojTija8&t=0s.

13. Ethan Yazzie-Mintz and Kim McCormick, "Finding the Humanity in the Data: Understanding, Measuring, and Strengthening Student Engagement," in *Handbook of Research on Student Engagement* (New York: Springer, 2012), 756.

14. Sir Ken Robinson, "How Do Schools Kill Creativity?," NPR TED Radio Hour, October 3, 2014, https://www.npr.org/2014/10/03/351552772/how-do-schools-kill-creativity.

15. Tony Wagner and Ted Dintersmith, *Most Likely to Succeed: Preparing Our Kids for the Innovation Era* (New York: Scribner, 2016), 58.

16. Wagner and Dintersmith, *Most Likely to Succeed*, 265.

17. "Imagination," *Psychology Today*, accessed October 7, 2024, https://www.psychologytoday.com/us/basics/imagination.

Chapter 2

1. Jonathan Vespa, Lauren Medina, and David M. Armstrong, *Demographic Turning Points for the United States: Population Projections for 2020 to 2060* (Washington, DC: U.S. Department of Commerce, 2018), updated February 2020, 6, https://www.census.gov/content/dam/Census/library/publications/2020/demo/p25-1144.pdf.

2. Véronique Irwin, Ke Wang, Julie Jung, Erika Kessler, Tabitha Tezil, Sara Alhassani, Alison Filbey, et al., *Report on the Condition of Education 2024* (Washington, DC: National Department of Education, May 2024), 16, https://nces.ed.gov/pubs2024/2024144.pdf.

3. Robert Sam Anson, *Best Intentions: The Education and Killing of Edmund Perry* (New York: Knopf Doubleday, 2011), 155.

4. Anson, *Best Intentions*, 187.

5. "culture," *Merriam-Webster.com,* 2020. https://www.merriam-webster.com/dictionary/culture (April 20, 2020).

6. "climate," *Merriam-Webster.com,* 2022. https://www.merriam-webster.com/dictionary/climate (March 21, 2022).

7. Anson, *Best Intentions*, 154–155.

8. Larke N. Huang, Rebecca Flatow, Tenly Biggs, Sara Afayee, Kelley Smith, Thomas Clark, and Mary Blake, *SAMHSA's Concept of Trauma and Guidance for a Trauma-Informed Approach* (Rockville, MD: Substance Abuse and Mental Health Services Administration, 2014), https://ncsacw.acf.hhs.gov/userfiles/files/SAMHSA_Trauma.pdf.

9. Johnmarshall Reeve, "A Self-determination Theory Perspective on Student Engagement," in *Handbook of Research on Student Engagement*, ed. Sandra L. Christenson, Amy L. Reschly, and Cathy Wylie, Springer Science + Business Media, 149–172, https://doi.org/10.1007/978-1-4614-2018-7_7.

10. Jonathan Shaw, "Rigor with Joy? Rethinking the American High School," *Harvard Magazine* (May–June 2019), https://www.harvardmagazine.com/2019/05/high-school-rigor-reform.

11. Douglas Richesson, Iva Magas, Samantha Brown, and Jennifer M. Hoenig, *Key Substance Use and Mental Health Indicators in the United States: Results from the 2022 National Survey on Drug Use and Health* (Rockville, MD: U.S. Department of Health and Human Services, 2023), https://www.samhsa.gov/data/sites/default/files/reports/rpt42731/2022-nsduh-nnr.pdf.

12. "Wisqars Leading Causes of Death Visualization Tool," CDC.gov, accessed September 10, 2024, https://wisqars.cdc.gov/lcd/?o=LCD&y1=2022&y2=2022&ct=12&cc=ALL&g=00&s=0&r=0&ry=0&e=0&ar=lcd1age&at=groups&ag=lcd1age&a1=0&a2=199.

13. Zara Abrams, "Stress of Mass Shootings Causing Cascade of Collective Traumas," American Psychological Association, *Monitor on Psychology* 53, no. 6, updated October 27, 2023, 20, https://www.apa.org/monitor/2022/09/news-mass-shootings-collective-traumas.

14. Carl G. Jung, *Alchemical Studies: The Collected Works of C. G. Jung*, vol. 13 (Princeton, NJ: Princeton University Press, 1983).

15. Anson, *Best Intentions*, 105.

16. Mark 8:36, King James Version of the Bible.

Chapter 3

1. Jim Harter, "In New Workplace, U.S. Employee Engagement Stagnates," Gallup.com, January 23, 2024, https://www.gallup.com/workplace/608675/new-workplace-employee-engagement-stagnates.aspx#.

2. Véronique Irwin, Ke Wang, Julie Jung, Erika Kessler, Tabitha Tezil, Sara Alhassani, Alison Filbey, et al., *Report on the*

Notes

Condition of Education 2024 (Washington, DC: National Department of Education, May 2024), 37, https://nces.ed.gov/pubs2024/2024144.pdf.

3. Aileen M. Pidgeon, Nyketa L. Davies, and Peta Stapleton, "Factors Influencing University Students' Academic Experience: An International Study," *International Journal of Multidisciplinary Perspectives in Higher Education* 2 (2017): 1–8, https://files.eric.ed.gov/fulltext/EJ1227520.pdf.

4. Danielle Dreilinger, "What Is KIPP Through College, and How Does It Work?," NOLA, updated July 7, 2021, sec. Education, https://www.nola.com/news/education/what-is-kipp-through-college-and-how-does-it-work/article_18d6a170-8c62-51b1-9d05-68d3031a12b7.html.

5. Casandra E. Harper, Rachael Orr, and Ellen Bara Stolzenberg, "Demographics, Purpose, and Dreams: Predicting Entering College as an Undecided Major Student," *NACADA Journal* 43, no. 2 (December 2023): 136–145, https://doi.org/10.12930/NACADA-22-42.

6. Dreilinger, "What Is KIPP Through College, and How Does It Work?"

7. Ted Dintersmith, *What School Could Be: Insights and Inspiration from Teachers Across America* (Princeton, NJ: Princeton University Press, 2018), 91.

8. Carol S. Dweck, *Mindset: The New Psychology of Success* (New York: Ballantine, 2006), 189.

9. "Bachelor's Degrees Conferred by Postsecondary Institutions, by Field of Study: Selected Academic Years, 1970–71 through 2021–22," Digest of Education Statistics, accessed September 10, 2024, https://nces.ed.gov/programs/digest/d23/tables/dt23_322.10.asp.

Don't Let School Get in the Way of Education

10. "Steve Jobs 2005 Commencement Address," Stanford Report, June 12, 2005, https://news.stanford.edu/2005/06/12/youve-got-find-love-jobs-says/.

11. "Steve Jobs 2005 Commencement Address."

12. *State of the American Workplace Report,* "Employee Engagement Insights for U.S. Business Leaders" (Gallup, 2013), 12–13.

13. Xinhua, "Chinese Wisdom in Xi's Words: Cultivating People Is Like Growing Trees," *China Daily,* updated March 31, 2022, https://www.chinadaily.com.cn/a/202203/31/WS62453c75a310fd2b29e546b0.html.

14. "The Philosophy of the Classroom in One Generation Will Be the Philosophy of Government in the Next,'" Barry Popik.com, October 7, 2015, https://www.barrypopik.com/index.php/new_york_city/entry/the_philosophy_of_the_classroom_in_one_generation.

15. Scotty Hendricks, "Why Socrates Hated Democracy, and What We Can Do about It," Big Think, October 7, 2017, https://bigthink.com/politics-current-affairs/why-socrates-hated-democracy-and-what-we-can-do-about-it/.

16. Hank Rubin, "Education: Democracy's Midwife," *The New York Times,* August 10, 2006, https://archive.nytimes.com/www.nytimes.com/ref/college/coll-adp-rubin.html#:~:text=Just%20as%20a%20free%20press%20helps%20ensure%20the,generation%2C%20and%20education%20is%20its%20midwife%22%20%28John%20Dewey%29.

17. In a letter to George Wythe (August 13, 1786), Jefferson said: "Preach, my dear Sir, a crusade against ignorance; establish and improve the law for educating the common people." Thomas Jefferson, "Letter from Thomas Jefferson to George Wythe," August 13, 1786, National Archives: Founders Online, https://founders.archives.gov/documents/Jefferson/01-10-02-0162.

18. Madonna Murphy, "Plato's Philosophy of Education and the Common Core Debate" (conference paper, Association for the Development of Philosophy Teaching [ADOPT], De Paul University, Chicago, IL, April 25, 2015), 5, https://files.eric.ed.gov/fulltext/ED559997.pdf.

19. Dr. Martin Luther King Jr., "The Purpose of Education," Stanford, 1947, accessed October 7, 2024, https://kinginstitute.stanford.edu/king-papers/documents/purpose-education#fn1.

20. Michael Onyebuchi Eze, "I Am Because You Are," *The UNESCO Courier*, updated April 20, 2023, https://courier.unesco.org/en/articles/i-am-because-you-are.

21. Chris Cameron, "These Are the People Who Died in Connection With the Capitol Riot," *The New York Times*, updated October 13, 2022, https://www.nytimes.com/2022/01/05/us/politics/jan-6-capitol-deaths.html.

22. Denisa R. Superville, "Students Are Walking Out to Protest Gun Violence. What Should School Administrators Do?," *Education Week*, February 27, 2018, https://www.edweek.org/leadership/students-are-walking-out-to-protest-gun-violence-what-should-school-administrators-do/2018/02.

23. "Voting and Registration in the Election of November 2020," Reported Voting and Registration by Age, Sex, and Educational Attainment: November 2020, 18 to 24 Years, U.S. Census Bureau, April 2021, https://www.census.gov/data/tables/time-series/demo/voting-and-registration/p20-585.html.

24. The quotation by Aristotle is disputed. Steve and Dan Fouts, "It Is the Mark of an Educated Mind to Be Able to Entertain a Thought Without Accepting It," Aristotle–Critical Thinking, *The Teach Different Podcast*, n.d., https://teachdifferent.com/podcast/it-is-the-mark-of-an-educated-mind-to-be-able-to-entertain-a-thought-without-accepting-it-teach-different-with-aristotle-critical-thinking/; Alexander Atkins, "Famous Misquotations:

It Is the Mark of an Educated Mind…," Atkins Bookshelf, May 1, 2019, https://atkinsbookshelf.wordpress.com/2019/05/01/famous-misquotations-it-is-the-mark-of-an-educated-mind/.

25. "Why didn't Socrates try to escape his death sentence?," *Encyclopedia Britannica*, accessed October 7, 2024, https://www.britannica.com/question/Why-didnt-Socrates-try-to-escape-his-death-sentence.

Chapter 4

1. Daryl Cagle, "Grades 1960 and Now," Cagle.com, updated October 7, 2024, https://cagle.com/cartoonist/cagle/2010/04/27/77685/grades-1960-and-now.

2. Véronique Irwin, Ke Wang, Julie Jung, Erika Kessler, Tabitha Tezil, Sara Alhassani, Alison Filbey, et al., *Report on the Condition of Education 2024* (Washington, DC: National Department of Education, May 2024), iii, https://nces.ed.gov/pubs2024/2024144.pdf.

3. "About," Metairie Park Country Day School, accessed October 14, 2024, https://www.mpcds.com/about.

4. Peter Kernion, administrator, Jesuit High School, interviewed by author, February 6, 2018.

5. "Jesuit High School: Mission," Jesuit NOLA, accessed April 22, 2023, https://www.jesuitnola.org/about/mission/; Kernion interview, 2018.

6. Sean J. Goodwin, principal, and Kenneth St. Charles, president, St. Augustine High School, interviewed by author, February 8, 2018.

7. Monty Fontenot, school head, and Jenni Vega, principal, Northlake Christian School, jointly interviewed by author, February 21, 2018.

8. John T. Curtis, headmaster, John Curtis Christian School, interviewed by author, February 27, 2018.

9. "Mission Statement," Archbishop Shaw High School, accessed April 22, 2023, https://www.archbishopshaw.org/about/mission-statement/.

10. Father Louis Molinelli, headmaster, Archbishop Shaw High School, interviewed by author, February 27, 2018.

11. "Educational Philosophy of Don Bosco," Salesians of Don Bosco, accessed October 7, 2024, http://www.donboscowest.org/pedagogy/preventive-system.

12. Jack S. Truxillo, headmaster, Cabrini High School, interviewed by author, March 5, 2018.

13. "Our Mission," Cabrini High School, accessed April 22, 2023, https://cabrinihigh.com/mission.

14. Denis Rousselle, superintendent, Plaquemines Parish School Board, interviewed by author, June 19, 2018.

Chapter 5

1. "education," *Merriam-Webster.com*, https://www.merriam-webster.com/dictionary/education (May 30, 2024).

2. "educate," *Merriam-Webster.com*, https://www.merriam-webster.com/dictionary/educate (September 2, 2024).

3. *Oxford Learner's Dictionary*, "Education - Etymology (Word Origin)," accessed June 9, 2023, https://www.oxfordlearnersdictionaries.com/us/definition/english/educate.

4. Kevin Hall, *Aspire: Discovering Your Purpose Through the Power of Words* (New York: William Morrow, 2010), 46.

5. Kevin Kruse, "Zig Ziglar: 10 Quotes That Can Change Your Life," Forbes, updated July 8, 2013, https://

Don't Let School Get in the Way of Education

www.forbes.com/sites/kevinkruse/2012/11/28/zig-ziglar-10-quotes-that-can-change-your-life/?sh=6b7e398726a0.

6. Dr. Anane Olatunji, "Broccoli Education vs. Pumpkin," YouTube, accessed October 7, 2024, https://youtu.be/-JCgcV2iqJQ.

7. Oprah Winfrey, "Oprah Winfrey on Career, Life, and Leadership," YouTube, accessed October 7, 2024, https://www.youtube.com/watch?v=6DlrqeWrczs.

8. Stephen R. Covey, "Part 1: Paradigms and Principles," in *The 7 Habits of Highly Effective People: Powerful Lessons in Personal Change* (New York: Free Press, 1989), 17.

9. Covey, "Part 4: Renewal," in *The 7 Habits of Highly Effective People: Powerful Lessons in Personal Change*, 295.

10. George Bernard Shaw, *Back to Methuselah* (1921, Project Gutenberg 2004), Volume 2, Act 1, https://archive.org/stream/backtomethuselah13084gut/13084.txt.

11. "Percentage of Public School Students Enrolled in Gifted and Talented Programs, by Sex, Race/Ethnicity, and State or Jurisdiction: Selected School Years, 2004 through 2020–21," National Center for Education Statistics, accessed October 7, 2024, https://nces.ed.gov/programs/digest/d23/tables/dt23_204.90.asp.

12. A. N Rinn, R. U. Mun, and J. Hodges, *2020–2021 State of the States in Gifted Education* (National Association for Gifted Children, 2022), https://cdn.ymaws.com/nagc.org/resource/resmgr/2020-21_state_of_the_states_.pdf.

13. *2016 Gallup® Student Poll: A Snapshot of Results and Findings* (Washington, DC: Gallup, 2017).

14. Katherine Ellison, "Being Honest About the Pygmalion Effect," *Discover*, October 28, 2015, https://www.discovermagazine.com/mind/being-honest-about-the-pygmalion-effect.

Chapter 6

1. *Matilda*, directed by Danny DeVito (Sony Pictures Entertainment, 1996).

2. Sarah Fine, "Schools Need Teachers Like Me. I Just Can't Stay," *The Washington Post*, August 9, 2009, sec. Outlook, https://www.washingtonpost.com/wp-dyn/content/article/2009/08/07/AR2009080702046.html?sub=AR.

3. Judy Willis, "The Neuroscience of Joyful Education," *Engaging the Whole Child* 64 (Summer 2007), https://www.psychologytoday.com/sites/default/files/attachments/4141/the-neuroscience-joyful-education-judy-willis-md.pdf.

4. Hilary G. Conklin, "Toward More Joyful Learning: Integrating Play Into Frameworks of Middle Grades Teaching," *American Educational Research Journal* 51, no. 6 (December 1, 2014), https://doi.org/10.3102/0002831214549451.

5. Yinmei Wan, Meredith Ludwig, Andrea Boyle, and Jim Lindsay, "The Role of Arts Integration and Education in Improving Student Outcomes," *State Education Standard* 20, no. 1 (January 2020): 36–41, https://eric.ed.gov/?id=EJ1241600; Daniel H. Bowen and Brian Kisida, "Investigating the Causal Effects of Arts Education," *Journal of Policy Analysis and Management* 42, no. 3 (Summer 2023): 624–647, https://doi.org/10.1002/pam.22449.

6. Linda F. Nathan, "Joyful Learning at Scale: Immersing Students in the Arts," *Phi Delta Kappan* 101, no. 8 (April 2020): 8–14, https://doi.org/10.1177/0031721720923514.

7. Stacey Boyd, "Extracurriculars Are Central to Learning. Subjects Such as Art, Music, and Foreign Languages Have Long-Lasting Benefits," *U.S. News & World Report*, April 28, 2014, https://www.usnews.com/opinion/articles/2014/04/28/music-art-and-language-programs-in-schools-have-long-lasting-benefits; Katie Reilly, "Is Recess Important for Kids or a Waste of Time? Here's

What the Research Says," *Time*, October 23, 2017, https://time.com/4982061/recess-benefits-research-debate/.

8. Anane Olatunji and Allison Paige, "Liking and Learning Mathematics: The Data Analysis Project" (unpublished manuscript, 2007), typescript.

Chapter 7

1. "affirmation," *Merriam-Webster.com,* https://www.merriam-webster.com/dictionary/affirmation (January 19, 2024).

2. Kevin Hall, *Aspire: Discovering Your Purpose Through the Power of Words* (New York: William Morrow, 2010), 174.

3. Laura I. Rendón Linares and Susana M. Muñoz, "Revisiting Validation Theory: Theoretical Foundations, Applications, and Extensions," *Enrollment Management Journal* 5, no. 2 (Summer 2011): 15, https://www.laurarendon.net/wp-content/uploads/2021/07/rendon_munoz_revisiting_validation_theory.pdf.

4. Oprah Winfrey, "Oprah's Commencement Speech to Harvard University," Oprah.com, May 30, 2013, https://www.oprah.com/owners/read-oprahs-harvard-commencement-address.

5. Laura Huang, *Edge: Turning Adversity into Advantage* (New York: Portfolio, 2020), 18–19.

6. Huang, *Edge*, 19.

7. Rendón Linares and Muñoz, "Revisiting Validation Theory," 15.

8. Robert Windrem, "US Government Considered Nelson Mandela a Terrorist until 2008," NBCNews.com, December 7, 2013, https://www.nbcnews.com/news/world/us-government-considered-nelson-mandela-terrorist-until-2008-flna2d11708787.

Chapter 8

1. "Student's Classroom Rant Goes Viral," CNN.com, May 10, 2013, https://www.cnn.com/videos/us/2013/05/10/pkg-viral-student-rant.wfaa.

2. Johann Wolfgang von Goethe, from *Oxford Essential Quotations*, ed. Susan Ratcliffe (Oxford Press, 2018), accessed October 7, 2024, https://www.oxfordreference.com/display/10.1093/acref/9780191866692.001.0001/q-oro-ed6-00004900.

3. Kevin Hall, *Aspire: Discovering Your Purpose Through the Power of Words* (New York: William Morrow, 2010).

4. Hall, *Aspire*, 71–73.

5. Marva Collins and Civia Tamarkin, *Marva Collins' Way: Returning to Excellence in Education* (New York: TarcherPerigee, 1990), 22.

6. Collins and Tamarkin, *Marva Collins' Way*, 78.

7. Collins and Tamarkin, *Marva Collins' Way*, 1.

8. Collins and Tamarkin, *Marva Collins' Way*, 155.

9. Collins and Tamarkin, *Marva Collins' Way*, 87.

10. "Marva Collins (Part 1)," *60 Minutes* (CBS, 1995), https://www.youtube.com/watch?v=h8b1Behi9FM; Richard J. Herrnstein and Charles Murray, *The Bell Curve: Intelligence and Class Structure in American Life* (New York: Free Press, 1996).

11. Henry Gradillas and Jerry Jesness, *Standing and Delivering: What the Movie Didn't Tell* (New York: R&L Education, 2010).

12. "Making a Difference: Jaime Escalante," *NBC Nightly News*, March 31, 2010, YouTube, accessed October 8, 2024, https://www.youtube.com/watch?v=IM6blsMhPRQ.

13. Ramón Menéndez, dir., *Stand and Deliver*, Warner Brothers, United States, 1988.

14. Gradillas and Jesness, *Standing and Delivering*, 11.

15. "State Expectations for Graduation Matter and Differ More than You Think," Achieve.org, August 2018, https://www.achieve.org/graduation-requirements-matter.
16. Malcolm X and Alex Haley, *The Autobiography of Malcolm X* (New York: Grove Press, 1987).
17. Gradillas and Jesness, *Standing and Delivering*, 45–46.

Chapter 9

1. Postman, *The End of Education* (New York: Knopf Doubleday, 1995), https://archive.org/details/end_of_education/page/n57/mode/2up.
2. United to Rise (website), accessed October 8, 2024, https://unitedtorise.org/about/our-history/.
3. Talib Madyun, executive director, United to Rise, phone interview by author, March 22, 2024.
4. "YOUR Experience: A Day in the Life at YOUR Community Center," United to Rise, YouTube, accessed October 8, 2024, https://www.youtube.com/watch?v=y9RYK4cb5Y8.
5. Betsy Cohen, executive director, Youth Communication, video call meeting interview by author, June 5, 2024.
6. Youth Communication (website), "Testimonial by Lori Krane, Principal & Educator," accessed October 8, 2024, https://youthcomm.org/our-supporters/.
7. "Rejecting My Role Model," Youth Communication, accessed October 8, 2024, https://youthcomm.org/story/rejecting-my-role-model/.
8. Anane Olatunji and Allison Paige, "Liking and Learning Mathematics: The Data Analysis Project" (unpublished manuscript, 2007), typescript.

9. Tony Wagner and Ted Dintersmith, *Most Likely to Succeed: Preparing Our Kids for the Innovation Era* (New York: Scribner, 2016).

Chapter 10

1. Abraham Maslow, "Chapter 4: A Theory of Human Motivation," in *Motivation and Personality* (New York: Harper & Row, 1954), 35–58. Although Maslow's theory of hierarchy of needs has developed over the years, the discussion here focuses on the concept of self-actualization, which I believe remains relevant for the FACES framework.
2. Mike Oppland, "8 Traits of Flow According to Mihaly Csikszentmihalyi," PositivePsychology.com, December 16, 2016, https://positivepsychology.com/mihaly-csikszentmihalyi-father-of-flow/.
3. Oprah Winfrey, "Oprah Quote on Passion and Purpose," Oprah.com, accessed October 8, 2024, https://www.oprah.com/quote/oprah-quote-on-passion-and-purpose.
4. Napoleon Hill, "Desire," in *Think and Grow Rich* (New York: TarcherPerigee, 1937), 19.
5. John C. Maxwell, *The 15 Invaluable Laws of Growth: Live Them and Reach Your Potential* (New York: Center Street, 2012), 22.
6. Darren Hardy, *The Compound Effect: Jumpstart Your Income, Your Life, Your Success* (New York: Vanguard Press, 2012), 134.
7. Stephen R. Covey, "Part 1: Paradigms and Principles," in *The 7 Habits of Highly Effective People: Powerful Lessons in Personal Change* (New York: Free Press, 1989), 15–20.
8. Anthony Robbins, "Morning Motivation," Robins Rise, December 16, 2024, 17 min., 29 sec., https://www.youtube.com/watch?v=MoKdZ3PBavI.

9. Jim Rohn, "If You Don't Design Your Own Life Plan, Chances Are You'll Fall into Someone Else's Plan, and Guess What They Have Planned for You? Not Much," Quotespedia, accessed November 22, 2024, https://www.quotespedia.org/authors/j/jim-rohn/if-you-dont-design-your-own-life-plan-chances-are-youll-fall-into-someone-elses-plan-and-guess-what-they-have-planned-for-you-not-much-jim-rohn/.

10. James Clear, *Atomic Habits: Tiny Changes, Remarkable Results* (New York: Avery, 2018), 253.

11. Stephen R. Covey, "Sharpen the Saw," in *The 7 Habits of Highly Effective People: Powerful Lessons in Personal Change* (New York: Free Press, 1989), 287; "Jim Rohn: You Need to Work Harder," YouTube, Jim Rohn Channel, 53:02, December 7, 2023, https://www.youtube.com/watch?v=UnGH_Da2_TA.

12. Mike Penner, "Woody Hayes: In Death, He's Still a Winner," *Los Angeles Times*, March 12, 2007, https://www.latimes.com/archives/la-xpm-2007-mar-12-sp-briefing12-story.html.

13. John C. Maxwell, *Failing Forward: Turning Mistakes into Stepping Stones for Success* (New York: HarperCollins, 2007), 2.

14. Hardy, *The Compound Effect*, 11.

Conclusion

1. Tara Garcia Mathewson, "Teacher Expectations Top List of Effects on Student Achievement," K-12 Dive, July 5, 2016, https://www.k12dive.com/news/teacher-expectations-top-list-of-effects-on-student-achievement/422029/; Stephanie Pierce, "The Importance of Building Collective Teacher Efficacy: Leadership and Accountability Are Critical to Student Access," *Leadership Magazine*, September/October 2019, https://leadership.acsa.org/building-teacher-efficacy#:~:text=Collective%20teacher%20efficacy%20is%20%E2%80%9Cthe%20perceptions%20of%20teachers,on%20students%E2%80%9D%20

%28Goddard%2C%20Hoy%2C%20%26%20Woolfolk%20
Hoy%2C%202000%29.

2. Brian M. Stecher, Deborah J. Holtzman, Michael S. Garet, Laura S. Hamilton, John Engberg, Elizabeth D. Steiner, Abby Robyn, et al., *Improving Teaching Effectiveness: Final Report: The Intensive Partnerships for Effective Teaching Through 2015–2016* (Santa Monica, CA: RAND Corporation, 2018), https://www.rand.org/pubs/research_reports/RR2242.html.

3. While there is evidence that Albert Einstein used this quote, the name of its originator is debatable. "Not Everything That Counts Can Be Counted," Quote Investigator, July 6, 2019, https://quoteinvestigator.com/2010/05/26/everything-counts-einstein/#google_vignette.

Index

A

ABC (A Better Chance) scholarship program and community, 47–55
academic rigor. *See* rigor
achievement
 and rigor versus well-being, 41–42
 study on teacher effectiveness and, 200–201
Adams House sculpture (Harvard University), 141
administrators, educational, 199–200
Affirmation, in FACES framework
 author's experience of, 143–147
 combining with challenge, 151–152, 158
 key points, 147
 nine ways to provide, 136
 overview, 125–127
 relation to other features of framework, 182, 193
 research related to, 127–131
 and self-determination theory, 169
 Teresita's story, 131–136
agency, 169. *See also* Expression, in FACES framework
Ali, Muhammad, 5
alienation from school. *See also* Broccoli Model of Education
 author's journey, 9–10

book overview, 6–8
career-related effects of, 66–67
causes of, 4–5
citizenship-related effects of, 67–71
college-related effects of, 59–63
consequences of, 3–4
general discussion, 197–198
how to use book, 10–13
overview, 1–3
solution to problem of, 5–6
alienation from self, 67
Amoako, Darryll S. (Suli Breaks), 27
Anson, Robert, 37, 38, 40, 46
Archbishop Shaw High School (New Orleans area), 83
Aristotle, 71
arts education, 113–114
Aspire (Hall), 90, 126, 152–153
Atomic Habits (Clear), 190
autonomy, in self-determination theory, 42, 169. *See also* Expression, in FACES framework

B

The Bell Curve (Herrnstein and Murray), 156

Don't Let School Get in the Way of Education

Best Intentions (Anson), 37, 38, 40, 46
Beyoncé, 128
bias breeding blindness, in leadership, 44–45
Bliss, Jeff, 26–27, 111–112, 205
Bosco, John, 75, 83
Broccoli Model of Education
    and author's experience in prep school, 47–55
    career-related effects of, 58, 64–67
    citizenship-related effects of, 58, 67–71
    college-related effects of, 58, 59–63
    consequences on school experience, 22–26
    and diversity in schools, 35–36
    Edmund Perry's experience, 37–38
    experiences of actual students, 26–28
    far-reaching consequences of, 57–59
    general discussion, 55
    key points, 33, 55, 72
    leadership and, 44–47
    need for change, 30–32
    overview, 7–8, 17–22, 87
    versus Pumpkin Muffin Model, 93–95, 98–99, 198–199
    researcher comments on, 28–30
    rigor versus well-being in, 41–44
    school climate and, 39
    school culture and, 39–41
bullying, school responses to, 24–26
Burgess, Dave, 82
business model, applying to education, 31, 42

C

Cabrini High School (New Orleans area), 83
calculus, example of challenging youth in, 156–159
Capitol attack (2021), 69
career planning
    lack of attention to in schools, 62
    role in Success, 189
career-related effects of conventional education, 58, 64–67
careers, versus jobs, 111

Carter, Jimmy, 137
Challenge, in FACES framework
    advocating for one high standard for all, 160–164
    combining with Affirmation, 151–152, 158
    Connection and Direction, 151–153
    exemplary models of, 153–159
    general discussion, 159–160
    key points, 164
    overview, 149–151
    relation to other features of framework, 182, 193
    and self-determination theory, 169
character, 68–69
citizenship-related effects of conventional education, 58, 67–71
Clear, James, 190
cognitive development, focus on, 98
Cohen, Betsy, 173
college
    effects of conventional education on, 58, 59–63
    Steve Jobs's views on, 64–66
Collins, Marva, 154–156, 160–161, 163, 199
competence, in self-determination theory, 42, 43, 169
compliance, focus on, 43
The Compound Effect (Hardy), 191
Conklin, Hilary, 112–113
Connection and Direction strategy for challenging youth, 151–153, 159–160
control. *See* Expression, in FACES framework
controversial issues, teaching about, 67–71
conventional education. *See* Broccoli Model of Education
Covey, Stephen R., 96–97, 140, 188, 190
creative approach to schooling. *See* Pumpkin Muffin Model
creativity, effect of education on, 28–29, 30
critical thinking, 68–71
Csikszentmihalyi, Mihaly, 183
cultural differences, 53, 146–147. *See also* Affirmation, in FACES framework

232

Index

D

Data Analysis Project (DAP), 118–121
De Pree, Max, 149
debt, student, 60–62
Deci, Edward L., 42
degrees, shelf life of, 63
DEI (diversity, equity, and inclusion) issues, 35–36. *See also* Affirmation, in FACES framework
democracy, education and, 68
Dewey, John, 68
Dillard University, 129
Dintersmith, Ted, 29–30, 61–62, 109
Diogenes, 57, 58
direction
    lack of in students, 59–63
    as strategy for challenging youth, 151–153, 159–160
diversity, equity, and inclusion (DEI) issues, 35–36. *See also* Affirmation, in FACES framework
"Do Schools Kill Creativity?" (Robinson), 28–29, 77
Dweck, Carol, 62

E

Earth, Wind & Fire, 137
Edge (Huang), 129–130
education. *See also* alienation from school; Broccoli Model of Education; FACES framework; "passion propels performance!" paradigm; Pumpkin Muffin Model; schools addressing emotional development
    career as taking priority over, 64
    categories of curriculum and instruction in, 160–162
    defining, 89–91
    disconnect between self-actualization and, vii–ix
    moving toward emotional fulfillment, 6–7
    process of, 93–99
    purpose of, 91–92, 182
educational administrators, 199–200
Educational Testing Service, 157

effective teachers, study on, 200–201
Einstein, Albert, 30, 201
emotional well-being. *See also* Fun, in FACES framework; schools addressing emotional development
    author's experience in prep school, 47–55
    as foundation of human achievement, 42
    moving education toward emotional fulfillment, 6–7
    need to promote both rigor and, 45–47
    pursuit of rigor at expense of, 40, 41–44
    school culture and, 40–41
    school's neglect of, 4–5, 18–22, 24–26. *see also* Broccoli Model of Education
empowerment. *See also* Expression, in FACES framework; Success, in FACES framework
    in FACES framework, 193
    as purpose of education, 92, 182
engagement. *See also* schools addressing emotional development
    and Broccoli Model of Education, 22, 23
    envisioning educational system increasing, 99–100, 101
    importance to school leaders, 77, 79
enjoyment of learning. *See* Fun, in FACES framework
enthusiasm, role in education, 90–91
Escalante, Jaime, 156–159, 160–161, 163–164, 200
ethnicity-based educational institutions, 128–129
expectations, high, 151, 158. *See also* Challenge, in FACES framework
Expression, in FACES framework
    cultivating, 176–178
    key points, 179
    overview, 167–168
    relation to other features of framework, 182, 193
    significance of, 169–170
    United to Rise example, 171–173
    Youth Communication example, 173–176

F

FACES (Fun, Affirmation, Challenge, Expression, and Success) framework. *See also* Affirmation; Challenge; Expression; Fun; Success
  experiences inspiring, 201–205
  general discussion, 191–193, 199
  overview, 5–6, 8, 102–103, 104
  potential value of, 200–201
feelings, school's neglect of, 4–5, 18–22, 24–26. *See also* Broccoli Model of Education; emotional well-being
The 15 Invaluable Laws of Growth (Maxwell), 190
Fine, Sarah, 110–111, 199–200
fire, education as kindling of, 89–91
flow state, 183
Ford, James, 125
Fun, in FACES framework. *See also* FACES framework
  DAP effect, 118–122
  key points, 123
  overview, 109–112
  relation to other features of framework, 181–182, 193
  research related to, 112–114
  ways to make learning fun, 114–118

G

Garfield High School (Los Angeles), 156–159
Gates, Bill, 64
Geer, Ann, 51
gender-based educational institutions, 128–129
gifted, viewing all youth as, 100–102, 163–164
Goethe, Johann Wolfgang von, 151
Gomes, Peter J., 143–147
Gradillas, Henry, 158–159, 163–164
The Graduate (film), 59
graduation options, high school, 162
Guan Zhong, 67
guidance, role in challenging youth, 151–153, 159–160

H

Hall, Kevin, 90, 126, 152–153
Hardy, Darren, 187, 191
Harvard University, 137–138, 140–143
Hayes, Woody, 190
HBCUs (historically Black colleges and universities), 129
Hemingway, Ernest, 134
high expectations, 151, 158. *See also* Challenge, in FACES framework
high school graduation options, 162
High School Survey of Student Engagement, 22
Hill, Napoleon, 186
historically Black colleges and universities (HBCUs), 129
Huang, Laura, 129–130

I

"I Sued the School System" (Williams), 27–28
ideal education, 88. *See also* "passion propels performance!" paradigm
identity, affirming. *See* Affirmation, in FACES framework
intelligence, in current educational policy, 41–42

J

Jefferson, Thomas, 68
Jesuit High School (New Orleans area), 80–81
Jobs, Steve, 64–66, 67
jobs, versus careers, 111
John Curtis Christian School (New Orleans area), 82–83
"Joyful Learning at Scale" (Nathan), 113
Jung, Carl, 35, 45

K

kindling of fire, education as, 89–91
King, Martin L., Jr., 68
Kolderie, Ted, 17
Krane, Lori, 174

Index

L

leadership. *See also* schools addressing emotional development
  bias in as breeding blindness, 44–45
  need to promote both wellness and rigor, 45–47
learning, enjoyment of. *See* Fun, in FACES framework
Lincoln, Abraham, 67–68
loan debt, college, 60–62

M

Madyun, Joyce, 171
Madyun, Talib, 171
major, changing in college, 60–61
Mandela, Nelson, 137
Marva Collins' Way (Collins), 154, 155
Maslow, Abraham, 181, 182–183
mathematics
  exemplary model of challenging youth in, 156–159, 161
  making learning fun, 116–121
Matilda (film), 110
Maxwell, John C., 186, 190, 191
Mbiti, John, 69
mental health crisis among youth, 43
Metairie Park Country Day School (New Orleans area), 80
mind, education as cultivation of, 91
Mindset (Dweck), 62
Moralia (Plutarch), 89
Most Likely to Succeed (Wagner and Dintersmith), 29–30, 109
motivation. *See* FACES framework; "passion propels performance!" paradigm; self-determination theory
Murray, Charles, 156
music education, 113–114

N

Nathan, Linda, 113
National Assessment of Educational Progress (Nation's Report Card), 18, 19
national education reform initiatives and policies, 18–19
"The Neuroscience of Joyful Education" (Willis), 112
new paradigm for education. *See* "passion propels performance!" paradigm
nonacademic needs, schools addressing. *See* schools addressing emotional development
Northlake Christian School (New Orleans area), 81–82

O

Olatunji, Anane N.
  adolescent struggles of, 139–140, 142
  affirmation, importance of to, 143–147
  alienation from school observed by, 1–2
  importance of questions related to education, 88–89
  inspiration for FACES framework, 201–205
  personal journey of, 9–10
  prep school experience of, 47–55
  and role of fun in learning, 113
  and societal changes, 78–79
  struggles at Harvard University, 137–139, 140–143
  and Teresita's story, 131, 132–133, 134, 135
  views on conventional education, vii-ix
ownership of learning process. *See* Expression, in FACES framework

P

paradigm for education, new. *See* "passion propels performance!" paradigm
parents
  book as guide for, 11
  as reinforcing lack of direction in children, 62–63
passion
  and challenge, 152–153
  in Prosperity Principles for Youth Success, 186

role in career, 65
"passion propels performance!" paradigm. *See also* FACES framework
    definition of education under, 89–91
    demonstration of, 163
    educational process under, 93–99
    and FACES framework, 6
    key points, 103
    overview, 8, 12, 87–89
    purpose of education under, 91–92
    two steps toward, 99–102
people, in Prosperity Principles for Youth Success, 187
performance, in Prosperity Principles for Youth Success, 190. *See also* "passion propels performance!" paradigm
Perry, Edmund, 37–38, 46, 205
persistence, in Prosperity Principles for Youth Success, 190–191
personal interests, learning tailored to, 116–118, 121
personal responsibility, 155, 188. *See also* Expression, in FACES framework
perspective
    as aspect of self-knowledge, 96–98
    in Prosperity Principles for Youth Success, 188
Piaget, Jean, 98
planning, role in Success, 189
Plaquemines Parish School Board (New Orleans area), 84
Plato, 68
pleasure of learning. *See* Fun, in FACES framework
Plutarch, 87, 89, 90, 91
PMM. *See* Pumpkin Muffin Model
Postman, Neil, 167, 170
potential, nurturing, 170. *See also* Expression, in FACES framework
preparation, in Prosperity Principles for Youth Success, 189
presidential election of 2020 (U.S.), 69, 70
"Prince Ea" (Richard Williams), 27–28
private schools addressing emotional development, 76, 79
Prosperity Principles for Youth Success, 185–191

Pumpkin Muffin Model (PMM)
    versus Broccoli Model, 93–95, 98–99, 198–199
    characteristics of, 95–99
purpose
    lack of in students, 59–63
    in Prosperity Principles for Youth Success, 186–187
Pygmalion effect, 101

R

racism, 36, 140
real world, gap between school and, 4, 5
real-life experiences, learning through, 116–118
reform initiatives and policies, 18–19
relatedness, in self-determination theory, 42, 43, 169
relationships
    role in challenging youth, 151–153, 159–160
    role in Success, 187
Rendón, Laura I., 127–128, 136
Represent publication (Youth Communication), 174
responsibility, personal, 155, 188. *See also* Expression, in FACES framework
rigor. *See also* Challenge, in FACES framework
    need to promote both wellness and, 45–47
    pursuit of at expense of well-being, 40, 41–44
"Rigor with Joy?" (Shaw), 43
Robbins, Anthony, 188
Robinson, Ken, 28–29, 77
Rohn, Jim, 189, 190
Rosenthal, Robert, 101
Ryan, Richard M., 42

S

Safer, Morley, 156
St. Augustine High School (New Orleans area), 81
school climate, 39
school culture, 39–41

Index

schooling. *See* education
schools addressing emotional development
   challenges experienced in, 77–79
   inspiring ideas and insights from, 80–84
   interview questions for leaders of, 76–77, 79
   key points, 85
   limitations of study on, 79–80
   overview, 8, 75–76, 84–85
"Schools Need Teachers Like Me. I Just Can't Stay" (Fine), 111
SDT (self-determination theory), 42–43, 98–99, 128, 169
self, alienation from, 67
self-actualization
   disconnect between education and, vii–ix
   in FACES framework, 192, 193
   and success, 182–183
self-determination theory (SDT), 42–43, 98–99, 128, 169
self-expression, emphasis on at U2R, 172–173
self-knowledge
   danger of alienation from self, 67
   in Pumpkin Muffin Model, 96–98
   as starting point, 184, 192, 193
"The Seven Prosperity Principles for Youth Success", 185–191
The 7 Habits of Highly Effective People (Covey), 188
Shaw, George Bernard, 99
Shaw, Jonathan, 43
short term, helping students have success in, 184
skillful versus willful students, 170
small-group competition/collaboration, 118–121
social interaction, role in education, 98–99
society
   changes in, and excellence in education, 77, 78–79
   connection between education and, 67–71
Socrates, 68, 71

spiritual well-being, 11–12, 66. *See also* emotional well-being
Stand and Deliver (film), 158
standards, emphasis on in education, 18–21
student achievement, study on teacher effectiveness and, 200–201
student debt, 60–62
student well-being. *See* emotional well-being
Success, in FACES framework
   key points, 194
   overview, 181–184
   relation to other features of framework, 191–193
   Seven Prosperity Principles for, 185–191
   teaching youth to succeed, 184–185
Suli Breaks (Darryll S. Amoako), 27
surveying students
   to make learning fun, 121–122
   to promote Expression, 177
Swarthmore, Pennsylvania, author's experience in, 47–55
systemic racism, 36

T

Taylor, Robert, 59–60, 66, 183
Teach Like a PIRATE (Burgess), 82
teachers. *See also* Broccoli Model of Education; FACES framework; Pumpkin Muffin Model
   effectiveness of, study on, 200–201
   and excellence in education, 77–78
   resistance to change, 82
teams, making learning fun with, 118–121
technology, using as tool for good, 115
Think and Grow Rich (Hill), 186
"Toward More Joyful Learning" (Conklin), 112–113
trauma caused by educational experiences, 40–41
Tubman Educators
   exemplary models of challenging youth, 153–159

making learning fun, 115–116
overview, 10–11, 199
Tulane University, 129

U

underperformance
   alienation from school as breeding, 4
   author's experience with as adolescent, 141–143
United to Rise (U2R), 171–173
Urban League Street Academy (New Orleans), 116–118
U.S. Capitol attack (2021), 69
U.S. presidential election of 2020, 69, 70

V

validation
   author's experience of, 143–147
   importance of, 126–127
   key points, 147
   research related to, 127–131
   Teresita's story, 131–136
virtue, 68–69
voice and choice. *See* Expression, in FACES framework

W

Wagner, Tony, 29–30, 109, 178
Watkins, Arthur R., 90, 152–153
well-being. *See* emotional well-being
Westside Preparatory School (Chicago), 154–156
What School Could Be (Dintersmith), 61–62
Why I Hate School But Love Education (Amoako), 27
willful, becoming, 116, 163, 170
Williams, Richard ("Prince Ea"), 27–28
Willis, Judy, 112
Winfrey, Oprah, 96, 128, 183

Y

Youth Communication (YC), 173–176
Youth Organizations United to Rise (YOUR). *See* United to Rise

Z

Ziglar, Zig, 91
Zuckerberg, Mark, 64

Photography by Ecstatic Love Content

About the Author

ANANE OLATUNJI (ah-NAH-neh oh-lah-TOON-jee) has dedicated his career to improving educational outcomes for youth. To that end, he continues to serve the field as a consultant, speaker, trainer, and author, reaching audiences across the United States and abroad—in both English and Spanish.

Dr. Olatunji also is founder and president of **Align Education, LLC**, based in New Orleans. Under his leadership, the consulting firm has provided professional development and program evaluation services to organizations nationwide funded at more than $75 million.

Much of his success can be attributed to serving the field as both researcher and educator. For example, he not only has published in the *Harvard Educational Review*, but also taught students from kindergarten to college, including the daughter of **President Joe Biden**.

Prior to establishing his own firm, Dr. Olatunji served as an evaluator of educational programs at **Fairfax County Public Schools** in Virginia, where he received the superintendent's *Outstanding Performance Award* after one year of service. As assistant professor of education and director of public and private school initiatives at Dillard University in New Orleans, "Dr. O," as affectionately called by his students, was awarded the distinguished *Verret Teaching Prize* by the provost, who described his performance as "exceptional."

Dr. Olatunji's commitment to youth development is deeply rooted in his personal journey. Raised in a family of nine in an impoverished community in New Orleans, he nonetheless excelled academically. After graduating from high school in Pennsylvania through the A Better Chance scholarship program, he earned degrees in sociology and education from Harvard, Columbia, and Tulane University.

To learn about ways to implement the FACES framework in your educational program, or to invite Dr. Olatunji as a guest speaker, please visit: DrOinspires.com.

www.ingramcontent.com/pod-product-compliance
Lightning Source LLC
Chambersburg PA
CBHW030515080526
44586CB00011B/203